W9-DJK-091

For Love
of a Child

For Love
of a Child

STORIES
of
ADOPTION

WARNER MEMORIAL LIBRARY
EASTERN UNIVERSITY
ST. DAVIDS, PA 19087-3696

LISA MEADOWS GARFIELD

AGATE LAKE PUBLISHING
White City, OR

9-30-05

HV 875 .G33 2005
Garfield, Lisa M.
For love of a child

All reasonable efforts have been made to secure proper releases and permissions to use the stories and photographs in this book. Some names have been changed upon request. Neither the author nor Agate Lake Publishing is liable for any errors, omissions, libel, slander, misrepresentation or invasion of privacy.

Copyright © 2005 Lisa Garfield

All rights reserved. No part of this book may be reproduced or transmitted in any form or by any means, electronic or mechanical, including photocopying, recording, or by any information storage and retrieval system, without permission in writing from the publisher.

Published by Agate Lake Publishing
P.O. Box 2164
White City, OR 97503

Publisher's Cataloguing-in-Publication Data
Garfield, Lisa Meadows.

    For love of a child : stories of adoption / Lisa Meadows Garfield. —
    White City, OR : Agate Lake Publishing, 2005.

    p. ; cm.

    ISBN: 0-9754403-0-6
    Summary: An honest, compelling collection of true stories about
    the adoption experience from a variety of perspectives.

    1. Adoption—Anecdotes. 2. Adoptees—Anecdotes. 3. Adoptive parents—Anecdotes. I. Title.

HV875 .G37 2005   2004109156
362.734—dc22   CIP

Book production and coordination by Jenkins Group, Inc. • www.bookpublishing.com
Interior production by Barbara Hodge
Cover design by Kelli Leader
Front cover photo of Findley, the author's birth grandson
Back cover photo of the author with her adopted daughters (Photo by C. Mark Davis)

Printed in the United States of America
09 08 07 06 05 • 5 4 3 2 1

Dedication

*For all the children of the world
who are waiting to belong to a family*

Contents

Introduction

Stories of adoption are so full of human drama that they cannot help but touch us on a very deep level. Within these pages, you'll hear birth parents, adoptive parents, adoptees, and a birth grandmother tell their stories. These are real people, telling true stories. In fact, this is as Real as life gets. Adoption always involves pain, deep courage, fear, faith, joy, and above all—love of a child.

All adoption stories involve a child. In the adoption community, we usually speak of the adoption triad—a triangle composed of Child, Birth Parent, and Adoptive Parent. We normally identify ourselves with one side or another of the triad. But my experience with adoption—as the sister of an adopted child, an adoptive mother, and a birth grandmother—has softened those hard triangular corners. No matter what your experience or perspective, adoption is a circle—a circle of love—with a child at the center. And the circle includes many people besides the three key parties. Everyone who knows anyone who is part of an adoption story (and that's most of us) is part of the circle.

I wrote *For Love of a Child* because I know adoption, from the inside out. I am part of several adoption circles, the first of which began in...

1966

I was nine years old, the oldest of three children. Our family's Saturday morning ritual was to play Sandwich in my parents' bed. Dad was usually the "bread" on the bottom, and we would pile on top of him in varying order. "I'm the cheese!" someone would holler. "I'm the bologna!" Or, "I don't want to be the mayonnaise again!"

Before we got up to eat pancakes with blueberries and sour cream, my parents would always ask, "What do you want to do today?"

For weeks, the three of us had been responding in a robotic litany, "Go get our baby brother!" And every week, my parents would reply, "Not yet."

Until today. Today, they calmly responded, "Okay." It took a minute for the news to sink in. From a child's perspective, the wait to welcome our adopted brother home had been interminable. We had lost faith in our parents' assurances that he really would come. But as soon as we realized they were serious, that this indeed was the long-awaited day, we leapt out of bed with whoops and hollers, and scurried to get ready.

We knew this was a special day, so we dressed ourselves in our Sunday best, without parental prompting. I brushed my seven-year-old sister's hair and helped my four-year-old brother tie his shoes. We were ready in ten minutes. We didn't even ask about pancakes with blueberries and sour cream.

I did think to ask, "Are we going to name him Mitchell or Phillip?", the two names under consideration. "His name is Phillip Grant," announced my mother.

My sister piped up, "How old is he?"

"Just three weeks old," replied my father.

Pat and Helen arrived, family friends who had agreed to be the baby's godparents. Dad put the car bed and the stroller into the back of the station wagon. Mom came out the front door with a bulging diaper bag. The five of us piled into the car, and with Pat and Helen following in their car, we drove the half hour to the adoption agency, where we were to meet our baby brother.

We were ushered into a room that looked to me like a fancy parlor. There were soft sofas and soft music. All seven of us perched expectantly on the sofa and waited. And then... there he was, a fat little ball of a baby, with a head full of dark hair and pudgy little hands.

We took turns passing him around, feeding him bottles, touching his soft toes and tiny fingernails. At last, overstuffed and much jostled, Phillip threw up all over my mother's best dress. My sister and I were thrilled, since we got to take off his clothes, check out his roly-poly tummy, and dress him in clean clothes. Mom and Dad signed some papers, and we walked to the car with our new family member.

It soon became apparent to me that being the oldest of four came with definite pros and equally definite cons. I delighted in being allowed to take Phillip on walks in his stroller, to be handed the camera as designated photographer, to be appointed the one in charge. I liked the power of my position. I did not like being expected to change dirty diapers in the back of a moving station wagon, or, in later years, having to drag Phillip along when I went to meet my boyfriend. But he was my brother. And I adored him.

Phillip's adoption was never a secret, within the family or outside of it. But neither was it a topic of frequent conversation. It was simply an accepted fact, like his eye color or his body build. I never knew anything about his birth parents, and never thought to ask, even though I knew he must have had some. His adoption was never given any undue importance—it was just the way he came to us. Though Phillip was the only one of us adopted, none of us ever felt any differently about him than we did our other siblings. We were a bit jealous over the way our parents spoiled him, but even as children, we did not attribute that to his adoptive status, but rather to the fact that he was the baby. Besides, the three of us participated wholeheartedly in the spoiling!

Phillip grew up to be a gentle, generous, unpretentious man. I am proud and grateful to call him my brother...

Fast forward thirty years. I had graduated from college, traveled, worked at this and that. Married. Birthed four children, who now occupied most of my time and energy. I was just moving into that transition period in the middle of life, when you begin to rethink everything, question what your life is about...

1997

I had ignored it for years. At first, it was just a nudge, a fleeting thought that would pass through my mind like water through sand: *Adopt.* Then it began to come as a prick to my heart or a flooding warmth in my belly. I knew these signs. I knew they signified some sort of spiritual message, some divine directive. But I wasn't listening, and didn't want to.

Finally, the sheer frequency of these experiences compelled me to tell my husband, "Honey, I keep having the crazy notion to adopt." I was counting on him to nip this one firmly in the bud. So I was at once dismayed and excited when he responded, "Oh, no! Me too!"

We still weren't ready to listen. We made a list of reasons not to adopt: too old, too expensive, too many kids, too much hassle, too many years devoted to child-rearing. It was an impressive list. We recited it to each other in weak moments.

Life went on. I was heavily involved in family and community activities. I enrolled in graduate school and got a teaching license. But every few months, the idea to adopt would resurface, and we would go over our list again, to convince ourselves it was a bad idea. It wasn't working. It began to get tiresome.

Finally, we decided, "We're groping in the dark here. Let's call a few agencies and get some real information and that will stop these silly promptings." We decided that IF we were to adopt, we would want an infant—and quickly—so we picked out a local international agency and got on their mailing list. Just in case.

The agency newsletters began to arrive each month, during a year of extreme stress. My graduate program was intense and time-consuming; grandparents began dying, in quick succession; our teenage son was struggling with drug abuse. I did not have time even to read the mail. But when that newsletter would come, I would sit and read the entire thing, cover to cover. I wept through most of it, not because I felt sorry for the orphaned children, and not because I felt compelled to save the world by adopting a child. I actually couldn't tell you why I wept, but I did notice that the newsletters were the trigger, and I recognized my reaction as another sign. Something big was brewing in my soul.

My husband and I had some long talks about priorities, about commitment, about how to build a life of value. We made another list, *Why We Should Adopt*, to counterbalance the first. But the only thing we could think of to put on it was: "It feels right."

In the end, as always, that was enough. The feeling was deep, even revelatory. We were in accord. We were ready to commit. We called the agency for an application.

During the long process of deciding to adopt, we had come to believe that our family was missing two girls, so we applied to China, since they had lots of baby girls available for adoption. But just as our application was submitted, China began a massive reform of their adoption policies and procedures. It quickly became apparent that, given our circumstances, it was going to be a long wait, with no guarantees. We were feeling too old to wait. The agency suggested, "How about Guatemala? We can find your baby girls much quicker there."

We didn't care where they came from. Our only concern was to find the "right" little girls, the two we felt were destined to be in our family. By this time, we had completely shifted from "control mode" to "faith mode" so we were open to whatever happened. We agreed, "Sure, let's go to Guatemala."

It was Saturday morning, just a few weeks later. Julie, our counselor from the agency, called and began to chat amiably. This was not unusual, so it took me a minute to realize, "Julie, it's Saturday! You never call on Saturday! Why are you calling on Saturday?"

"You have a baby daughter. She's eleven days old. Cute little thing, judging from this picture I have," she calmly announced.

I felt myself melting, right there in the kitchen. All the left-over doubt and fear was washed away by a wave of peace so profound I knew it would sustain me through whatever happened on the rest of this journey. Childbirth is more physically demanding than adopting, and the emotion is all tangled up with the bodily experience. To hear that I was a mother again—to a baby girl three thousand miles away—excluded me physically, but it allowed the emotion of the experience to stand sharply on its own, naked as a newborn babe.

Her birth mother had named her Julia, then had left her in the hospital where she was born. Who knows what circumstances prompted such a decision? I credit her for making a plan that ensured her daughter's safety and health. Julia was taken to a foster home run by an expatriate from Ohio, and there she stayed for nine-and-a-half long months.

The wait was agonizing. Every couple of months, we'd get new pictures and post them on the refrigerator. We named our new daughter Julia Grace and included her in all our family plans and prayers. We set up the crib and shopped for baby clothes and bottles.

Family and friends threw a surprise shower for Grace, though she still wasn't home yet. Because her birth parents could not be located, her case went through two court proceedings—one to free her legally for adoption, and the other for the actual adoption. Then the Guatemalan legal system shut down for six weeks for Christmas. The judge was sick for another several weeks. Our agency underwent some administrative changes, so we got a new adoption coordinator halfway through the process, half a continent away.

I tried to be patient. I tried to walk that fine line between being a pest and effectively advocating for my child through the adoption agency. I wasn't very good at it. I just wanted my baby home. Even though I hadn't even met my daughter yet, my heart was drawn to her every single moment. It felt entirely wrong to be separated from my child. Having birthed children, I knew what it felt like to be tightly bonded to a baby. This felt exactly the same.

Finally, all the legal work was complete and it was time to go pick up our daughter. My husband and I flew to Guatemala City and there in our hotel room, we met little nine-month-old Grace for the first time. She was old enough to be wary of us, but within a week, she must have decided that we were worthy of her trust, because from then on, she acted like she owned us. We spent a day at her foster home, snapping pictures of the people and places in her early life, then another day at the United States Embassy, securing her visa. We arrived at our home airport exhausted and ecstatic, like we'd just run a marathon. Grace's older siblings latched onto her immediately, reminding me of when Phillip came home to us. My oldest son, Garrett, responded to Grace with especially deep feeling, as though she were the embodiment of her name. She is a happy, gentle soul—an essential, delightful part of our family…

Over the next couple of years, we had children coming and going. We immediately applied for our second Guatemalan daughter, who was born early in the year 2000. After we'd received our referral and posted the photo of our beautiful, tiny brown baby on the refrigerator, I settled in for the long, heart-wrenching wait. But things went so smoothly that we were able to bring Gloria home at five months old. She arrived full of spit and vinegar, and while I'm still questioning why, of my six children, my "wild child" should come last, I can see in her a strong, world-changing woman, and I consider it an honor to be her mother.

In the meantime, my son, Garrett, had left for college with high hopes and a new focus for his life. My husband and I breathed a huge sigh of relief to see him back on track, so I was unprepared for the phone call we received just two weeks after he'd arrived at school in Hawaii...

1998

"I'm in big trouble," Garrett moaned through his tears.

"What's the problem?" I asked, alarmed at his emotional state.

"Katherine's pregnant."

Garrett was nineteen. Katherine was seventeen. They had only recently broken up, after a long, intense relationship. In this new chapter of his life, becoming a father was not part of Garrett's plan, at least not at this point.

Katherine, who was still in town, called next, feeling distraught and alone. My heart was breaking for both of them. I felt an immediate compassion and concern for them, because I knew what a huge impact this would have on their lives, not only in the next few months, but always. I knew that no matter what they decided to do, it would be a difficult experience.

Over the next few weeks, I listened a lot and offered feedback, as the two of them weighed their options. Both of them called me daily, seeking advice. From the beginning, my position was one of support and encouragement, but I refused to relieve them of the responsibility that was theirs to deal with the situation they had created. It would have been easy for Garrett to run. He wasn't carrying the baby. He was three thousand miles away, and the relationship was over. And it would have been easier, in many respects, for Katherine to simply handle it on her own and not bother with involving Garrett. Instead, both of them faced this shared challenge with a maturity and selflessness rare in people so young.

We talked our way through the various options—marriage, abortion, teenage parenthood. Garrett and Katherine rather quickly settled on adoption as the best choice for their circumstances. Despite pressure from her family to abort the baby, and her own support of abortion rights, Katherine concluded, "I just can't do it." Since my husband and I were looking for our second adoptive daughter at the time, we discussed whether this might be our baby, but none of us felt any kind of peace about that idea.

Katherine decided to join Garrett in Hawaii for a few months, to work more closely with him in finding an adoptive family for their child. Money was tight, and they both worked to keep themselves housed and fed and healthy. They worked with an attorney and chose a family in Louisiana to parent their child. But after several months, the arrangement fizzled, so at seven months pregnant, Katherine came home with no adoptive family and no prospects.

Time was short. Both Garrett and Katherine were still firmly committed to adoption, but were beginning to panic that nothing had been arranged yet. Katherine, a determined and proactive person, immediately contacted a local open adoption agency and began to gather information. She passed some literature about open adoption to me, commenting, "Now this seems like the best way to do an adoption. What do you think?"

I was unsure about the whole philosophy and practice of open adoption, having had such good experiences with closed adoption. Garrett, too, was wary of the tangled relationships that seemed to loom in an open adoption. But I couldn't help but notice that, for the first time in this whole process, I did feel a gut-level joy at the possibility of maintaining a relationship with this little person that I already loved. This was my first grandchild, and the thought of losing him had been a constant grief. The spark of joy introduced by the idea of open adoption conflicted with my worries over what I presumed would be a stressful, complicated relationship with my grandson's adoptive family. But an open adoption clearly seemed the best option for the child. It took some time to come with peace with all of this, but Katherine was a persuasive "research team leader," and as her surrogate partner in Garrett's absence, I became converted to the concept.

It was a new thing for me, to be on the birthing side of the adoption triad. I knew from experience how emotional it is to be the adoptive parent, trying to find the child you know is meant to be yours. But this was just as intense, trying to identify the family that we knew was meant to raise our child. It was like we were trying to find the exact puzzle piece that would make our family circle complete.

Katherine called one day and announced excitedly, "I think I've found them!" She told me she hadn't responded to any of the "Dear Birthmother" letters in the book the agency provided. But when they handed her a picture of a brand new applicant—Hans and Joell—she immediately felt something shift, like coming home.

We got copies of their entire dossier and shipped one off to Garrett. I took one home and put it under my pillow to sleep on. Katherine talked to her family and friends, then met with Hans and Joell. Garrett called and advised me, "Go meet them. Tell me everything."

So one crisp autumn day, I drove with Katherine to the agency to meet Hans and Joell, armed with Garrett's photo album and his list of questions. I was nervous. It is such a monumental task, choosing parents for a child you feel responsible for and love so deeply. As Garrett's proxy, I did my best to represent him honestly and accurately. Hans and Joell and Katherine and I shared pictures and family stories and dug into hard questions about values and lifestyles.

Everyone's intuition was on high alert. I had learned to trust Katherine's remarkable intuitive abilities, and I knew to trust my own. In the end, you go with your gut. But there were things to talk through, because open adoption, in its best form, involves a long-term relationship, to be developed and agreed upon right at the start. There are no rules, no right or wrong ways to work it out. And in the beginning, you're working on just theory and commitment, without the benefit of personal experience. There are other people's stories to lean on and learn from, but that's not your baby, not your life. This was real, and we all felt the significance of the process, the impact our choices would have. We all felt much of the other's pain—the pain of infertility and the pain of relinquishing the right to parent your own child. That empathy for each other's experience helped bond us. It became a deep, shared commitment to do our very best, whatever our role, to give this child the life he deserved.

I called Garrett with my positive report. Sent more packets. Met with Hans and Joell several more times, in less formal settings. After all the setbacks in this journey, it was hard to trust our collective sense that this was good, that we had finally found our family. Garrett said, "Go for it." Katherine told Hans and Joell, "We would like you to parent our child."

Garrett came home from college in December and spent a lot of time with Katherine, Hans, and Joell, talking through issues and preparing for the birth. Though he had no reservations about Hans and Joell as adoptive parents for his child, it took quite some time—even well beyond the birth—for him to sort out his feelings about the open adoption. I saw less of Katherine now, as her support system grew, though she did join us for Christmas Eve and played the perfect pregnant Mary in our family Christmas pageant.

My phone rang early in the morning on January 6th, and I heard Katherine report, "I've been feeling funny all night—not really contractions, but something, so I called the midwife and she said to come over to the hospital. So that's where I'm headed."

"Okay, call us when you know what's happening," I replied. Then I roused Garrett to report the news and went back to bed. Garrett hugged the portable phone under his covers and waited.

An hour later, the phone rang again and I heard Garrett talking to Katherine. He came into my bedroom and calmly reported that Katherine was dilated to eight centimeters and was going to have a baby soon. I sat bolt upright.

"Eight centimeters! And she didn't even know she was in labor?! Get over there! Go! Now! I'll follow you in a few minutes!"

I love the birthing experience. I love it when I am the one birthing, and the few births I have witnessed have been amazing, moving experiences. This particular birth, with all the joy and sorrow that was wrapped around it, was truly a sacred experience. Katherine labored with calm and courage in a large round tub filled with warm water. Garrett held her up and whispered encouragement. Her mother, who had come from out of state for the birth, coached her breathing. Her grandmother and I, along with Hans and Joell, provided vocal and non-vocal support. The midwife and the nurse monitored her progress. A sense of purpose permeated the room as we gathered around Katherine for the final stage. I held Joell's hand and watched my son across the circle focus all his attention and love on the wondrous task at hand. With a final huge effort, Katherine pushed the baby into the waiting hands of the midwife and into the welcoming hearts of his family, all of us united in love for him, then and forever.

Katherine cradled her new son, then passed him to Garrett. Around the circle he moved, each of us blessing him in our own way. I didn't realize how much emotion I was holding in until the midwife—a sensitive and caring woman—hugged me on her way out of the room, and I suddenly melted into a puddle of loss and grief right there in her arms. Over her shoulder, I watched my son hold his firstborn close to his heart and whispered, "How can we let him go?"

The next two days were the hardest of all. Everyone was on emotional overload. Garrett stayed with Katherine in the hospital, the two of them caring for little Findley around the clock. The baby stayed wrapped in the blanket I had made for Garrett at his birth almost twenty years previously. The rest of us visited in shifts—Hans and Joell, Katherine's family, our family, including Garrett's four siblings, who loved Findley and felt a great loss, as well.

The pictures from that time show me holding Findley, beaming. I don't remember feeling as happy as I look. But even though I knew he wasn't really ours, he was mine in that moment, snug in my arms, certain family features already apparent on his brand new face, that little face permanently imprinted on my heart.

The strange thing was, in the midst of processing this huge loss, I was also very excited for Hans and Joell. I understood what it was like to welcome your adopted child home, to have him finally here, finally yours. To become a parent through adoption is a deep emotional experience, and having been in a similar position, my empathy for them was high. Because we were all in this together from the beginning—Findley's birth family and his adoptive family—we shared all of the emotions of the experience, the pain and the loss, the joy and the hope.

The open adoption experience allowed me to see and feel and understand adoption as a total experience, an intricate web of giving and receiving, of joy and loss. The love and courage required of Garrett and Katherine to walk the path they did has made them champions in my eyes. And the generosity and grace that I always feel from Hans and Joell, as we continue our adoption journey together, has made them fast friends. There is still a low-level layer of grief in my heart, even five years later, that I suspect will always be there. But there is incredible joy, as well, in watching my grandson grow up strong and smart, in seeing him secure in the love of his parents, his little brother, and his extended family. And his heart is open to his "Grandma Lisa," just as mine will always be open to him.

Perhaps you, too, love a child in an adoption circle. Maybe you are the child. Perhaps you feel drawn to find your child, or a family for your child. Or you are walking with a friend on their adoption journey. Honor that feeling—that stirring of the heart that leads you into what is Real. Stories of adoption are more than just tales of loss and courage and joy. They are stories of the heart. To love a child is to know the heart of God.

Lisa Meadows Garfield

Cheri

"I have no problem at all with being adopted. I know it was meant to be. I'm perfectly at peace with it, and I always have been."

My birth mother became pregnant by her husband's best friend—and that's how I came to be. Her husband was away in the army at the time, and when he came home and found out about the pregnancy, he forgave her, but told her, "I don't think I can treat this child the same way I would if I knew it was my own." I think that was big of him, actually, to be so considerate of me. So they decided to place me for adoption.

My parents found me through an adoption agency in Georgia. They had seen a show on television about hippies having babies, then giving them up for adoption when the children were toddlers. My parents thought, "Let's adopt one." After discussing it further, they decided to adopt a brand new baby instead. They were forty years old at the time, which was the agency's cutoff age for adoptive parents of newborns. And they already had four living biological children. Luckily for me, it all worked out. So I'm the baby, the only blonde in the family, the only one adopted.

I came home when I was thirteen days old. I stayed in the hospital for a few days after my birth, then I went to the agency, then home to my family. That's a lot of moving in my first two weeks of life. The adoption agency told my mom that I would probably always have a hard time saying goodbye to people I love. And it's true, I do. It's not that I consciously worry that the person won't come back. But I used to stand at the door and wave for a long time when someone in my family left. I thought everyone was like that, until I talked to a friend who has both birth and adopted children. She told me her adopted kids do similar things, but not her birth children. So maybe it has something to do with those early experiences of loss.

My mom worried about being older than the other mothers, but it never mattered to me. I was nine years younger than my next sister, and my first nephew is eight years younger than me, so I grew up in the middle. My sisters were out of the house, mostly, when I was growing up. I was close to them, though, because they lived just down the street, and I would visit almost every day. I grew up knowing I was adopted, but I've never felt like being an adoptee is what defines me.

I'm very close to all my family. My mom is a warm, open person—everyone loves her. I've always told her everything. When I was in Junior High, she helped me through some issues with girlfriends and that really solidified our bond. My dad used to come visit me at college once a month, and he and I grew closer through those visits. I think the reason I've never had any real issues with being adopted is because my family is so close and because my adoption was never a secret. It was never made an issue in our home.

Even as a teenager, I felt fine about it. My cousin, though, who is also adopted, really struggled. She had a hard time figuring out who she was and why her birth mother didn't want her. She felt abandoned by her birth mother. But I never felt that way. I really didn't think about my birth parents much.

I haven't tried to meet them. I haven't felt any interest or need. My mom has asked me if I would like to try to find my natural parents, but I've always declined. I know people who have found their birth parents and some of them have a good relationship now. But I don't have any desire to find mine, and I think that's probably because I am so close to my family. I don't feel any lack in my life. If I discovered that my birth mother was looking for me, I would probably respond. But before I would agree to a meeting, I would make sure she understood that I already have a family that I love dearly. I would be willing to meet her, but I imagine our relationship would be more like a friendship.

If I could tell my birth parents anything, I would tell them not to regret giving me up. I know a lot of birth parents continue to wonder if they did the right thing. To give up a child is probably the biggest thing they'll ever do. But I have such a great life! I live by the motto "we're here to have joy," so why not have it? If I could, I would like to relieve my birth parents of any guilt, because there's no reason for it, in my mind. I'm grateful to them for my life, to be where I am, and to be who I am.

My mom told me this story about the day I came home:

The agency said we needed to take you back to the hotel for a day, to make sure all the family got along with you. They wanted us to be sure we wanted to keep you. I told them, "Oh, we already know we want her." But they insisted. So we took you back to the hotel and all your siblings were arguing over who got to hold you.

I had a dream that night. I saw a man in a white robe with a baby in his arms. I didn't notice him much because I was enthralled with the baby. He handed the baby to a lady sitting in a chair. I watched her as she hugged and kissed the baby, tears rolling down her cheeks. Then she brought the baby to me, placed her in my arms, and said, "She's all yours. Take good care of her."

I think this is the reason I have no problem at all with being adopted. I know it was meant to be. I'm perfectly at peace with it, and I always have been. I belong to such a great family, and I'm so grateful for that. It's all I need.

Erik

"One of the advantages of open adoption is that it keeps our children connected to the important people in their life."

We didn't know the first thing about adoption when we started on this journey. My wife, Susan, and I didn't marry until our late thirties. We tried to conceive in the usual fashion, but it wasn't working, so we went to a reproduction expert. He told us, "Your odds of having a biological child are about 3%. With all we can do, we can only double the odds." Rather than go through all that hassle and expense, we immediately decided, "Let's adopt, because that's what you do when you can't have a child."

I didn't have any problem with the idea of not perpetuating my own genes. Intellectually, I've thought about it, but emotionally, I haven't felt it as a loss. Adoption is very emotional. I've received so much back from being the father of my children, both giving and receiving love, that any loss I may have felt along the way is negligible. We joke about it now: "What's so great about our family genes that they should be perpetuated?"

We started investigating adoption agencies and discovered that an old friend of mine—an attorney—was very involved in the open adoption scene in Oregon. Because I knew him to be a great guy, I figured if he was involved, I could trust open adoption. So we dove in. I read one book on adoption, passed it to my wife, then we went to an informational seminar at Open Adoption and Family Services. At the end of the presentation, we asked, "Where do we sign up?" We didn't even have to discuss it. We just knew this was what we were going to do.

Another reason I was drawn to open adoption is because of the experience of my sister. When she was twenty, she had a baby and placed it for adoption, and she has never seen that child again. The pain that she has suffered because of that, even to this day—twenty-seven years later—was enough to turn me off. It was one of those big secrets in my family, and keeping a secret like that felt terrible. It was a huge loss for my sister. The only objection I had to adopting was the thought that I might be causing some birth mother to live a life of regret and uncertainty. I didn't want to be the cause of such pain. That was simply unacceptable to me. So the philosophy of open adoption was exactly right for me. All our fears were dismissed when we learned that our kids could have ongoing contact with their birth parents. It seemed so much more humane and sensible than what my sister had gone through.

We went through the orientation process, prepared our pictures and biographies, did all the paper work, joined the pool of about sixty prospective parents, and then we waited. We were one of a handful of couples in the pool that indicated we would accept a child of another race, or an older child, or a sibling pair. Those are tough choices. You have to honestly examine your own life and values. There are many correct answers to those questions, but they have to be right for you. We were pretty open in that regard. So as children like that became available, the agency would call us.

When these opportunities would come up, it would send us into complete turmoil. We'd get out the almanacs, call social workers, doctors, friends—anybody we could think of who might know something about the particular situation. Every little scrap of information got blown out of proportion, because as soon as we'd get one question answered, five or six more would pop up. We had a couple of these false alarms, but the birth mothers made other decisions, so those children did not become available to us.

The "real" call came as a result of the birth father's sister stepping in as an advocate for the child. Our first daughter, Christine, was taken into the custody of the State when she was about two years old. Her birth parents were very low functioning, living on the fringes of society. They suffered from drug and alcohol addictions and ran into minor trouble with the law on a fairly consistent basis. They were living a life that nobody would choose on purpose. It's often hard for us stable, middle-class, college-educated people to realize that there are a lot of people out there who just do not function well within our culture.

The State had put Christine in foster care and her aunt was worried about her getting lost in the system, so she pushed to resolve the matter. The court was about to terminate the birth parents' parental rights, and the only way they could continue any contact with Christine was through an open adoption. The birth parents couldn't deal with reading the biographies and trying to choose an adoptive family, so they told Christine's aunt, the birth father's sister, "You choose someone." She found our profile in the book of prospective parents and remarked, "These people look interesting to me. They look like the kind of people I could relate to."

The agency called us and announced, "You have a beautiful little girl." We went in immediately and they showed us a picture of a very pale little child with fluffy hair, sitting on a tricycle in a hallway. That was our first glimpse of our daughter. She was almost three years old and had been in foster care for ten months.

We then met with the birth parents, which was a tense situation. I felt so much uncertainty. I was nervous because so much was at stake. This was our dream, our money, our hearts—all of it tied up together. Of course, I really wanted the adoption to work, but you don't know until you go into it whether the birth parents are amenable or whether they'll fight the legal system. It's the tension of the unknown. In retrospect, I worried needlessly.

The mediation room was full of people. There were attorneys for every party, counselors, me and Susan, the birth parents—Paul and Staci, plus a friend of theirs who had come along and who didn't like us because we didn't go to the "right" church. But Paul countered, "Well, it's our decision and we like these guys." So we worked out an agreement and signed the papers. Staci was pretty quiet, and we couldn't help but notice that she was about six months pregnant.

The first time we met Christine was when we drove out to her foster home to see her. To ease the transition, the social workers had planned a two-week period of visits before we took her home with us. We were sitting in the living room with the foster parents, the State social worker, and the adoption agency counselor, waiting for Christine to come home from her morning preschool. She came in the door and her foster mother asked her, "Christine, do you know who this is?" She shouted, "New mom and dad!" and ran across the room and into our arms, like she was jumping off a sinking boat.

We would visit in the evenings every couple of days and play with her, give her a bath, tuck her into bed. It was hard on her, because she was ready to go home with us. Even though she liked her foster family, she completely accepted that we were her new family. We were scrambling to get her room set up, and one day when we were visiting, she saw her mattress in the back of our truck and asked, "Is that my new bed?" She wanted to sleep on it then and there. She was in tears every time we said goodbye. The agency accelerated the transition because she was adapting so well to us. And that's how Christine came to be ours.

We did not have any contact with Paul and Staci for about six months, because we were advised it would help Christine bond with us. We did know through the agency that they had had a baby girl named Jamie. We told Christine, "You have a baby sister. Your birth parents are going to take care of her, and maybe we'll meet her someday." The agency called after Christine had been home about nine months, and asked, "Would you like the chance to meet Jamie? She's available for adoption."

Susan immediately responded, "Yes! Let's get this kid out of foster care." But I was worried. I'd barely adjusted to having one child. What would two mean? What would it mean financially? What would it do to our time? And this baby was only six months old. I liked the fact that Christine had come to us already talking, because if something was wrong, she could tell us. My wife had a lot more experience with babies than I did, so she had no problem with Jamie's age. But I had no idea what to expect.

We decided to go meet Jamie. We were told this was just a visit, that the paperwork had not been signed yet. Well, as soon as we saw this cute little baby, we said, "Of course we'll take her." The counselor replied, "That's good, because the judge has just freed her for adoption, so you have to take her right now."

We were on our lunch break from work. We had nothing for a baby—no car seat, no crib, no diapers, no bottle. She came with one bottle, the clothes she was wearing, and an extra diaper. I made a quick trip to borrow a car seat and a portable crib, and to buy some supplies, while my wife called friends who had children a little older to see what we could borrow or scrounge. In just a few days, we had a mountain of donated baby stuff in our front hall. I stopped in at work to say I wouldn't be back in that afternoon, then I picked up Christine at daycare and told her, "You have a new baby sister. Let's go home right now and meet her."

There were two other siblings born after Jamie, and we were asked if we wanted to adopt them, too, but we decided two was enough. We weren't getting any younger. The other two, a boy and a girl, were placed with two different families and we get together with them about twice a year, so the kids can know their siblings. The three families have a joint birthday party each year for everybody. It's so interesting to see the four kids together—they all look alike! When they're with each other, it's like they've always been together. That's one of the advantages of open adoption—it keeps our children connected to the important people in their life.

Paul and Staci call us from time to time. Their lives are so unstable that it's hard for us to keep track of them. We visit them when we can arrange it. Sometimes we meet at McDonald's or the ice cream parlor. But other times, we've gone to see them in homeless shelters or rehabilitation centers. We set up some strict guidelines for ourselves regarding the visits. If we ever feel that a situation is not good for the kids, we'll simply leave. But that's never happened. Paul and Staci haven't ever done anything questionable with the girls present. They have a real affection for them. They have made some effort to be part of their lives, but we are losing track of them as time goes by.

How do you tell your children about their birth parents, when their lives are so messed up? Our party line is, "They have a lot of troubles." We parcel out information as the kids need it. We try not to shock them too much, but we don't hide anything. We pledged to keep no secrets, so we tell them as much of the truth as they can handle.

It's sad, though. One Christmas, we were driving to a homeless shelter to visit Paul and Staci. Jamie was one year old and Christine was four. Christine was explaining to her little sister who these people were: "Jamie, we're going to see our birth parents. They love us very much, but they have problems."

I never imagined that my family would come together this way, but it's so perfect. We're just a normal family. How you spend your time together matters much more than whether your children are a genetic copy of you. It feels entirely natural to me. And I think that's true for the girls, as well. Christine has always talked very openly about her adoption, and I think she will always be a strong advocate for adoption. Already, she tells us, "When I grow up, I'm going to adopt."

I can't even think of a downside to adoption. It's an act of faith to have children, and whether you birth them or adopt them, there are no guarantees about their health or their intelligence or their compassion or anything. You just have to put yourself out there and deal with whatever comes.

Epilogue

One day we received a phone message from Paul. I replayed it three times to be sure I'd heard it right. "Did you hear about Staci? If not, my condolences." Staci had died in her sleep at age thirty.

Staci's life was shadowed by sadness. She endured domestic violence, drug abuse, prison time, homeless shelters and suicide attempts. At the time of her death, she was in a residential treatment center. She went up to her room one night and never came down.

Staci loved her kids as much as any mother could. She quietly shared her hope that her daughters would go places she'd never been. Her first question to us was always, "How are the girls?" But she couldn't raise them any more than she could save herself. Her death was the death of hope—hope that she'd recover, hope that she'd be happy, hope that her kids could know her better.

As a family memorial, we lit candles for Staci at the dinner table. The four of us each shared one thing we liked about her and one thing about her that made us mad, because anger swirled in our sadness. She loved to play on park swings; she didn't phone enough. She knew she was sick; she didn't stop drinking. She loved us; she didn't keep promises.

Staci's gifts to us were two strong, beautiful daughters who will explore a world she never knew. Because of open adoption, they'll grow up knowing three of their siblings. They know the truth about how their birth mom lived and died, although that's a hard truth for young hearts to hold. They know they can choose a different path from hers. And they understand that every life, however flawed, can bring beauty into being.

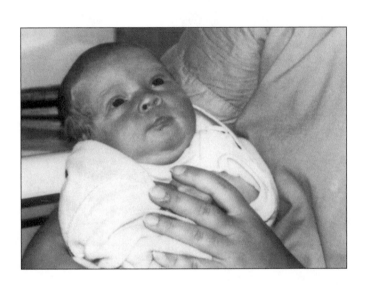

Donna

"The phone rang one summer day and when I picked up the receiver, I heard, 'Hello. You don't know me, but I'm your daughter.'"

I got pregnant in the usual way. When I was a freshman in high school, I went to band practice one night and fell madly in love with a drummer. He was two-and-a-half years older than me and we dated for a long time. But when my mother found out I was pregnant, she said we couldn't see each other anymore.

We were the usual inexperienced teenagers who thought it could never happen to us. My boyfriend had lots of interesting theories on birth control, like taking an aspirin while drinking a Coke. Actually, it's amazing that I didn't get pregnant sooner than I did. I was sixteen when it finally "happened" to me.

This was before the days of home pregnancy kits and I was too afraid to go to the doctor. But I knew I was pregnant about two months into it. My boyfriend wanted me to have an abortion right away, but this was not a good option for me. In the first place, it was illegal. And secondly, I really didn't want to. I was too young to know how I really felt about abortion, but I didn't like the whole idea of it. Besides, I would have had to find an abortionist out of the country, and I was a sixteen-year-old girl with no money and no contacts.

It was a scary situation. My boyfriend pretty much said, "You deal with it," so I did the really mature thing and ignored it, hoping it would go away or that he would change his mind and marry me. We talked about marriage, but he didn't want to get married. At the time, I was willing to marry him, but looking back on it, I realize that that was not a good option either.

In those days, pregnant girls either got married or gave their baby up for adoption. Those were the only real options. Nobody kept their baby. You either kept the pregnancy a big secret and went to live with relatives, had your baby, and gave it up for adoption—or you got an abortion somehow—or you got married. That's the way it was in 1972.

I didn't tell anyone I was pregnant, except for my boyfriend. My best friend never knew, and I was with her practically every day. When I was seven months pregnant, my mother began suspecting, but I denied everything. Then she took me to the doctor, and I couldn't get out of that. The doctor told my mother, "I know what the trouble is; she's pregnant."

Then came the Big Meeting between my mother, me, and my boyfriend. He came over to our house, and my mother asked him, "So what are your plans? Are you going to marry my daughter?" He told her he didn't want to get married, and my mother immediately went into her maternal protection mode. She told him that from that point on, he was not allowed to come to the house, or call me, or see me. He was totally cut off. She just laid down the law, so that was the end of that relationship.

I was so numb through all of this that I didn't even know how I felt. Besides being pregnant, I'd just lost my boyfriend. I walked around in a state of numbness all the time. I knew I had very few choices. I knew the whole thing was beyond my control now. I was very sad, very lonely, and very scared, but also very numb. I was just trying to get up every morning and get through the day. I don't remember feeling anything. It was a surreal existence.

The doctor who was treating me told my parents, "I'll handle the adoption for you if you'd like," and they agreed. Because I was already seven months pregnant, we didn't have a lot of time or options. It would have been silly to send me away at that point.

My doctor had a personal friend who wanted to adopt my baby. All I was told about the adoptive parents was that it was a doctor and his wife, that they were "good people," and that they couldn't have children. That's all I knew.

I found out years later that the adoptive father made some effort to see me. My doctor would tell him when I was coming in for appointments and he would wait in the hall to see me come in. He was actually on call at the hospital when the baby was born, so he was there within half an hour after she was born, to see her and hold her. But I didn't know that then, and I was not allowed any contact with the adoptive parents.

The birth was easy, physically. One Thursday morning, I was very pregnant, and by that afternoon, I had a baby girl. I stayed in the hospital for three days with her, because the law in Arizona at the time decreed that you couldn't relinquish parental rights before the baby was three days old.

The doctors and nurses were very nervous. I think they were afraid I would steal the baby or something. They treated me like I was a leper. I would ask them to bring me the baby, and they would say, "Oh, I don't know about that." I kept asking, with no result, so that first night, I finally got up, walked to the nursery, found my baby, and carried her back to my room. The nurses didn't know what to do. They stood there staring at me, wringing their hands.

She was a beautiful baby. She was a nice pink color, so I called her "Rose." I hadn't thought of a name beforehand, but that's just what I called her to myself. I never told anyone, because I knew that a lot of things were not my right or place to do. I didn't try to nurse her. I just held her in the bed, so she could feel my heartbeat, and I talked to her until she fell asleep. I must have fallen asleep, too, because when I woke up early in the morning, she was gone.

The only other time I had contact with her was the next day. I went to the nursery and they allowed me to sit in a rocking chair and hold her. Everybody tiptoed around us and whispered, but I didn't care. I just sat and rocked my baby.

On the third day, they took me into a room with lots of people that I didn't know. I signed the papers, relinquishing my parental rights. I never knew much about the mechanics of the adoption. I just signed the papers and it was done. I knew I had no other option, no other way to be sure my baby would be cared for.

Again, I was very numb. I tried not to think about what was happening. I don't remember agonizing over it, because I knew it was something that had to happen, something I had no control over. I had no power in this situation.

I was back in school on Monday. No one knew what had happened. I felt very alone for the rest of the school year and all through the summer. I never told anyone about it. What would be the point?

We never talked about it in my family, either. The day I came home from the hospital, it was like it never happened. We never spoke of it again. My extended family didn't know. There were times, during the last two months of my pregnancy, when my relatives would come over, and I was instructed to hide in my closet and stay there until they left. One time, my grandmother showed up unannounced and my parents panicked. I was standing in the kitchen when she knocked on the door, and my mother made me sit on a barstool at the counter, to cover up my stomach. My grandmother came in and started talking to me, but I didn't stand up until my parents made a quick plan to take her out to dinner and they left the house. The message to me was clear: *We do not talk about this. We do not tell anyone. We're just going to survive until it's over.*

I wasn't angry about that. I knew it wasn't my parents' fault. It was such a different world then, and I knew they were doing the best they could. I felt like I was the guilty party, that I deserved whatever happened. I deserved to lose her. For a long time, I thought that was my punishment for having sex and for getting pregnant. It wasn't my place to feel sorry for myself or to be angry. In a way, I felt like God's punishment for my sin was that I would never be allowed to have my baby. To even think otherwise would be like spitting in the face of God.

My last year of high school was actually very exciting. I hooked up with a new group of friends and was very involved in school activities. I didn't think much about the baby. Sometimes I'd see a baby that was about her age, and I'd wonder about her, but that didn't happen often. I just buried it all and went on with my life.

I had fun in college, too. I dated lots of people. I was very involved in journalism. But I went through some bad periods and was out of control for a long time. At the time, I made no connection between my behavior and the baby. But looking back, I realize I was trying to medicate myself to avoid the pain.

Then I met Jim and I knew the minute I saw him that I was going to marry him. He walked into a newspaper staff meeting and I started fumbling papers and giggling and acting silly. It was love at first sight.

Jim got me through a lot of bad stuff, most of which had to do with my feeling very unworthy of anything good. When we knew we would marry, I told him everything. I didn't want something that important to go unsaid between us. I remember wishing I were a virgin, but I obviously couldn't change that. He didn't care. Everything from that point on was very much uphill. We got married, I graduated from law school, and he continued in journalism. We had four children and built a beautiful life together.

I never told my kids about the baby or the adoption. I had no reason to think I would ever have any contact with her again, so what would be the point of telling them? I rarely thought about her. I was vaguely aware that she was getting older, but I wasn't counting the years.

Then one summer day, the phone rang. I picked up the receiver and heard, "Hello. You don't know me, but I'm your daughter." I was stunned. I didn't know how to respond. I was very cautious because of all the secrecy that had surrounded her birth. I asked her questions to try to figure out if it was really her. From the way she responded, I did believe it was my daughter. We talked for about an hour. She told me her name was Anne, which, of course, I had never known. She told me a little bit about her life and it sounded like she had had a wonderful life. She said all she knew of me was that I had been a high school student and that I had had no choice but to give her up. Basically, it was thank-you call. She told me, "I owe my life to you." She didn't ask to meet me.

I cried the whole weekend, while Jim sat with me. All of a sudden, I experienced this huge loss, because she was a real person now. She wasn't just a cute little baby doll that I had given to somebody, like a present you pick up off the shelf. That's how I had dealt with it all those years. I wasn't prepared for her to turn into a real person. But suddenly, she was very real. And she sounded so nice and so wonderful that I suddenly realized what I had lost. It was the first time I had ever really mourned about it. I couldn't get out of bed the entire weekend. I just cried and cried. But I'm a survivor, so on Monday morning, I got out of bed and went on with my life.

Years passed. I did think about Anne more often now. I knew a little bit about her life and I would wonder where she was, what she was doing. It did not occur to me to make contact. I did not want to meet her. I was very fearful of how it might affect my children. Would it make them think less of me? How would they feel about me keeping such a big secret from them? Would I suddenly be a fraud in their eyes? Would they wonder what else I hadn't told them? These were all big issues for me.

I knew my mother wouldn't approve, either, were I ever to pursue a relationship with Anne. Nor did I know how it would affect me. I didn't want to go there without knowing what would happen. I was worried about hurting myself and the people I loved. I thought it would be like having a picture of Disneyland and being told I could never go there, like someone saying, "There's this wonderful person out there, but you didn't ever get to be part of her life." I imagined it as constant pain, a constant reminder that I was an idiot for giving her up. At that point, I was having regrets about giving her up, because nowadays, keeping your baby is an option that I didn't have. It never occurred to me that meeting her could be a great thing.

The next phone call came nine years later. It was April Fool's Day, so I thought it was a prank. The call was from my old boyfriend, Anne's biological father. He told me he had met Anne and that I should meet her, too. I said, "No! I'm not going to do that!" I was still very much afraid. He said she had made contact with him and had come to Arizona to meet him and that it was a great experience. I wrote him a long, nasty e-mail, demanding, "How can you ask me to do this? It's too painful." But he kept talking about it, telling me what she was like, assuring me that she wasn't out to hurt me or to get anything from me, that she just wanted to meet me.

I had to go to Arizona for a legal conference, so I agreed to meet him for lunch. He showed me pictures of Anne, some from when she was a little girl and some current ones. It was the first time I'd seen what she looks like. She was so beautiful! There was something about the pictures—a gentleness in her eyes—that convinced me that meeting her just once might be okay.

I wrote a letter to Anne and told her, "If you want to meet, I'm ready." I went into it one toe at a time. I wasn't sure whether I would tell my kids about her, or what the future would look like. All I wanted then was to meet her—just once.

She flew in from the East and I flew down from the Northwest and we met in San Diego and spent a whole week together. It was a wonderful week! We got to know each other, and I concluded that there *is* something to biology. Here was this person that I didn't know at all, and yet, I felt an instant, overwhelming love for her. I felt like I knew her. I can't describe it very well, but I loved her immediately. It was amazing to discover that we're so much alike. It was an incredible, indescribable experience.

After that week, we kept in contact and met several times again. But I still hadn't told my children. That was still the big issue for me. I didn't want to hurt them, and I wasn't sure how they would react. There's no guidance on this, either. I couldn't just pick up an etiquette book and look up "what to do when your daughter suddenly re-enters your life."

It took me almost a year to decide to tell them. Actually, Jim was the one who convinced me I should. He had met Anne by this time, and his argument was, "I think she should be part of our lives, and I think our kids need to know. I don't think it should be a big secret." So we had a family meeting.

That was the hardest day of my life. Jim gathered the children and I came into the room and just started crying uncontrollably. We had just lost a friend to cancer, so my kids were pretty worried, because it was obvious that something big was up. They asked me if I had cancer, and I said, "No, but I need to tell you something that is really hard for me to say. I had a boyfriend in high school and we had a baby girl. I met her again recently, and I'd like her to meet you. I'd like her to be a part of my life and your life."

They were all very quiet for a long time, and I just held my breath. Then my boys said, "We have another sister? Cool! Can we go watch *The Simpsons* now?" One teenage daughter cried and asked a lot of questions. "Mom, that must have been so hard for you. How did you do that?" My oldest daughter didn't react much, but I imagine it's a pretty big deal to be suddenly displaced as the first child.

I talked to my mother next. I flew to Arizona and we spent four hours in our pajamas, discussing the whole thing. After all those years of silence, it was good to be able to talk about it, to let our Big Secret out of the closet. She told me what it had been like for her, why she'd handled it the way she did, and how she felt about it. But she does not agree that I should have any relationship with Anne and does not want to meet her. So we just leave that alone.

There have been bumps in the road, but overall, it's been a positive experience to reunite with my firstborn. My kids like her and she fits in well with our family. I have a good relationship with Anne that I feel would survive anything. It's a relationship unlike any I've ever had, so it's hard to describe. She's like a close friend, but more. She's not really my daughter, though. It doesn't feel like the relationship I have with my other daughters. We don't have all that history between us. Being a mother is more than giving birth—it's years of being together and loving each other and going through things together. It's experiencing life together.

I also have contact with Anne's adoptive parents. I've spent time with her mother and we call each other occasionally. She tells me that it has been a very positive thing for Anne to meet me, that she seems much happier, more content, not so lost. Her parents have been very supportive of Anne's relationship with me.

There's no question that meeting Anne again has been a positive thing in my life. It hasn't been painless, though. For example, when we were in San Diego, we were waiting in line to buy some food at Sea World. Anne was looking at the menu, and without thinking, said, "I want the Castaway Kid's Meal." We looked at each other and both burst into tears.

"You're not a castaway kid!" I said.

"I know."

Part of my pain is my regret over what Anne suffered as an

adolescent. Many adoptees go through an "adolescent adoption crisis" as they try to figure out their identity and purpose. Anne spent a lot of rocky years as an adolescent, and I have to wonder if I could have done things differently, to spare her that. But our relationship now is about one percent pain and ninety-nine percent joy.

I feel like a piece of me has been restored that I didn't even know was missing. I lived all those years, doing fine, doing wonderful things with my life, but there was a piece missing. It was like I had handcuffs on, but I got so used to doing things with handcuffs that I didn't notice. I didn't know that there was another choice.

I know now that I made the right choice. I chose to have her and to let her go, at great cost to myself and my family, but I know I did the right thing. All those years, I didn't really know that. I wondered if I should have had an abortion, or handled it differently somehow. Now I know that, given my circumstances, it was the best I could do, for her and for me.

All my feelings of guilt have changed, as well. I don't feel like God wants me to suffer. Originally, I thought that was part of my punishment, that I had lost her forever and that I would feel forever guilty about what I had done. I don't feel that way anymore. I'm not sure that I could have forgiven myself completely before now, because it wasn't real to me. She wasn't real to me. To know her as a real person, to see what I've contributed to the world, just by giving her life, brings me great peace.

Tom

"I had no wish to upset my relationship with my adoptive family, but I did feel a desire to reconnect with my birth family."

I was born in 1959, the seventh child of Norwegian immigrants. My father had come to America before World War II because he saw it as a land of great opportunity. He met and married my mother in South Dakota, scraped together some money to buy some property in Oregon, and built our family home on it with his own hands. The family survived financially mostly through his hard work and his ability to do things on his own, but we never had much money. My father was sixty-two years old when the eighth and last child was born. Then when I was six, my mother, who was twenty years younger than my father, got cancer and died.

After my mother died, a lot of people were concerned about the children in our family. There we were, eight kids with an older father who was trying to scrape by in construction. And my father's alcoholism only complicated things. There were times when I would come into the front room and find my dad passed out on the floor, a beer can spilled next to him. It was not a good situation.

I think he was depressed, on top of it all. He loved my mother, there's no doubt about that, and losing her was a big blow. My father had a lot of pride in his family and wanted to do the best he could. I knew he loved us. But he had his own struggles, and trying to carry on with all he had to deal with was just overwhelming.

Neighbors and church friends began suggesting to my father that he might want to put the younger children in foster care. That was the hardest thing in the world for him to do. But something had to change. There was a family next door willing to foster us, so the two youngest children—including me—moved in with the Ashfords. I lived there for a year and a half before people started asking about adopting us.

My sister, who is a year older than I am, had been staying with another family down the street. She was good friends with their daughter and was quite attached to the family already, so they adopted her. My youngest brother was adopted when he was two years old, but the family moved to California a few years later. I didn't see my brother again for twenty years.

My oldest sister was twenty-two at the time. This whole situation put her in a very difficult spot. She had to decide whether to stay near the family and play "Mom" or take the opportunity to ride off into the sunset with her new husband, who was finishing college in Wisconsin. She had seen my dad at his worst and she wanted a ticket out of there. So she chose to leave and never return, but that decision has haunted her ever since. It was especially hard on my older siblings to watch their younger brothers and sisters leave their life. They were hurting constantly, but felt powerless to do anything about what was happening.

My second oldest sister, Becky, was dating a young man named Jack. Jack's father knew a lot of people in the area. Of course, their family had an interest in making sure that we were all taken care of, so they started having family conversations about how to help our family. Becky eventually married Jack. And it was Jack's sister, who already had six children, that said, "I think I would have room for one of the boys." They expressed an interest in me because of my age, because I seemed a good fit for their family.

Nobody told me any of this. All I knew is that one summer day, when I was eight years old, I was invited to come to the Conrad's home to play with their kids. That's how it was explained to me. Well, that sounded fun to me, so I went. They lived across town, and when I got there, the children were all playing out in the front yard. I hopped out of the car and they yelled to me, "Hey, come on over and play!" Within five minutes, I was right in the middle of it all. There was an immediate connection. It felt perfectly natural to me. Of course, I wasn't thinking that they were going to be my new brothers and sisters. I was just having a great time.

I spent that night there, which was a little difficult. I lay in bed thinking about what a great time I had had that day, but wondering about my family. Although I liked it there at the Conrads, I wondered when I would get to go home. I loved my family. And I knew they loved me. I wasn't coming from a situation where there was no family, or where I was abandoned or abused. There was real love and concern in my family, even though I knew things were very unsettled. I could tell that something was up, but whatever was happening was happening behind the scenes, because no one talked to me about adoption, at that point. And I didn't ask.

The next day, the Conrads asked me if I would like to go back and get my stuff and spend the rest of the summer with them. I couldn't see any reason not to, so that's what I did. It opened up a whole new world to me. In my previous home, my whole world was all on one block. I played with the kids that lived on our street, and that was the extent of it. Here, there were all kinds of things going on—playing in the woods, baseball games, riding bikes and horses. It was like stepping up a degree.

At the end of the summer, Mr. and Mrs. Conrad invited me to stay and go to school with their kids. I was confused, because still, nobody was telling me much. I had very little contact with my birth family. My father and siblings showed up occasionally, to see how I was doing, but any contact was brief and not very informative. I was still wondering how my own family was going to fit into my new situation. I never vocalized any of this, but I was really worrying over it. I knew that if I did go back, I would probably go to the Ashfords, and that didn't seem any better than what I had here, so when they invited me to stay, I said, "Sure, that will be fine."

I spent the whole school year there, doing well in the third grade, carrying on as a Conrad, even though I wasn't an official family member. Then, at the end of the school year, they asked me if I would like to be a part of their family permanently. I remember thinking, "Since no one from my birth family is jumping in to object to this, and since I'm comfortable here, I guess this is what I'll do." So I became a Conrad.

I was unaware of the turmoil going on in my birth family. Everybody wanted what was best for the younger kids. Staying home with an alcoholic father or putting an extra burden on teenage siblings were obviously not good options. Nobody really wanted to see us adopted out, but it was something everyone felt forced into by the circumstances.

The transition into my new family was made harder by my change of name. They changed not only my last name, but my middle name as well, after my new grandfather. It was hard to think of myself as this new person. Of course, they asked me if I was willing, but I was too young to know any better. My middle names had been "Franklin Delano," names my father had chosen to honor one of his heroes. I had no idea who "Franklin Delano" referred to, so I thought, "If I have the chance to dump these ridiculous middle names, I'm going to do it." I let adults make my decisions. What else could a nine-year-old do?

Once the adoption was final, some walls sprang up between my new family and my old. My adoptive family had nothing but good intentions. They are good people with big hearts. But because they wanted me to be exclusively theirs, I think they subconsciously tried to keep me away from my birth family as best they could. And I can see why. That's what the culture of the time taught about adoption, that a clean break is best. It takes a huge heart to see beyond all that and let the birth family in. I don't think there was any agreement or arrangement made between the families. It became very difficult for me to maintain contact with my birth family, because the time between visits would be six months to a year and the visits would only last about an hour. Of course, I have a one-sided view of it, the view of a child taken away from his family, trying to adjust.

It was years before I could hear my birth mother mentioned and not immediately start crying. Being the only adopted child in the family was a bit of a sore spot with me. I did feel different, like a half-breed. I didn't know where I belonged. I felt like a Conrad and was dedicated to being part of the family, but at the same time, I knew I was a Morud, and I felt like I should be dedicated to them, too. If any of my new siblings got mad at me, they knew that if they mentioned I was adopted, they could really get to me.

My parents, however, were great. They treated me just like one of their own. One time, after a sibling spat, my mother pulled me aside, gave me a big hug, and said, "You know what, Tom? I have seven kids and you were the only one I was able to choose. All the others I got stuck with." That really comforted me. I understood that I wasn't just an "adopted" child; I was a "special" child. I take my hat off to her for being wise enough to know how to ease my mind.

Even though my adoption was a tender issue with me, I did feel genuinely loved and accepted by my adoptive family. I still felt a lot of grief over the loss of my birth family, but I'd come to grips with it pretty well. I thought of myself as a Conrad. I finally felt secure. I looked up to my mother and father and enjoyed my siblings. I felt like a real part of the family. So it was quite a blow when my father announced that he didn't love my mother anymore and that he wanted to create a new life for himself. I was eighteen years old. I'd been a Conrad for as long as I'd been a Morud. I'd watched my first family split apart, and now it was happening again.

My father left, and my mother went through a severe depression. It was a very difficult year. I was all set to leave for college, but my mom asked me if I would be willing to postpone school and be there for the family as the man of the house. So I stayed home and worked and tried to support my mom through her depression the best I could.

My parents' divorce was a big factor in my decision to seek out my birth family. I reasoned, "There's no real stability here either, and I've got blood relatives out there that I want to know." I had no wish to upset my relationship with my adoptive family, because I valued that family relationship. But I did feel a desire to reconnect with my birth family.

I was scared, though, because so much time had passed. Our lives were different. I was taught a different religion than most of them, so

I see things differently that way. I wasn't sure how they felt about me, because I hadn't made much of an effort to see them over the years. Were they mad at me? And what did we have to talk about?

I knew where all my birth siblings were, at least in a general sense, because of my connection with my sister, Becky. She was married to my adoptive mother's brother, so she became my aunt when I was adopted. That was pretty strange. My mom told me to call her "Aunt Becky," but it was too awkward to call my own sister my aunt. So for many years, I avoided calling her anything. Finally, when I turned eighteen, I approached her and said, "This is ridiculous. You're not my aunt. This has made me crazy for nine years, and I'm not going to call you 'Aunt Becky' anymore."

She said, "Oh, thank goodness!" And we made a pact right then—no matter what the circumstances, we would always be brother and sister.

My youngest sister, Leslie, had been adopted by her friend's family, one of our original neighbors. I had only seen her a few times during the past nine years. As it turns out, we both got jobs at JC Penney's, and the first day I went to work, several people said to me, "There's a girl that works upstairs that looks just like you." So I went upstairs to investigate, and there was Leslie. From then on, we started getting together to catch up on each other's lives.

One day, my birth father came and had lunch with me and Leslie. It was awkward, because we really didn't have anything to talk about. I never really knew him. I never felt angry at him about what had happened. I understood the circumstances, even at a young age. He died the following year, when I was living out of state. When I got the news, I didn't know how to react. I wasn't even sure who my "real" father was. I had lost both of my fathers, in a way. I didn't even come home for the funeral.

I'm still working to rebuild relationships with my birth family. I'm so used to not having them in my life that it's easy to do nothing. I think we all want to be part of each other's lives. But it takes effort. My older sisters do a fabulous job trying to keep us connected, and I know I don't give it half the effort they do. I have a stronger relationship with some siblings than I do with others, and I suppose that's natural.

That's true of my relationships with my Conrad brothers and sisters, as well. There are some, in both families, that I naturally take to, and those people feel like real siblings, no matter the blood relation. We share common interests. We do things together. We're friends. Those with whom I have a "real" relationship come from both families, about half and half. My desire is to have a great relationship with all of them. In my mind, they're all family.

I think it frustrates my mom that I want a relationship with my birth family. She's done a good job at incorporating me into the Conrad family. I consider her my "real" mom. But I think she wants me to be 100% hers, and even though I do feel that I'm a legitimate member of the family, I've never felt like I'm 100% Conrad. I never will be. This has always been my greatest challenge, trying to figure out who I am and who I belong to. It's a true identity crisis. Who am I? Where do I fit in?

Having lived the adoption experience, I have strong feelings about how things should be done, especially in a situation such as mine, where the child is older. If a child already has a family, a history, even though adoption may be the best course of action to provide a decent life for that child, the adoptive family ought to be mature enough and secure enough to let the child mingle with his first family and do what he needs to do to process what is happening. The child will be much healthier that way. He won't suffer as much. He may still have questions and concerns, but nothing will be hidden, and that will provide some much-needed security for the child. It takes a huge heart and an open mind to let the birth family in, to say, "This child had a life before me. He has memories and feelings and love for the other family." It is an injustice to keep the child away from the birth family. But it takes a generous person to be able to realize this, to allow the child access to his birth family, without feeling threatened.

In my case, there's always been a feeling of "us" and "them." The Moruds think they're the good guys—and they *are*—and the Conrads think they're the good guys—and *they* are. But they each think of the other family as just that—"other." There's no real conflict between them, but there's no contact either. At my fortieth birthday party, family members from both families showed up, but they didn't interact. In thirty-five years, they've never really come together. That makes me sad, because to me, they're all family.

There have been clear benefits to my adoption. I'm a very strong person, for one thing. Because of what I've had to deal with, I'm pretty solid. It would take a lot to shake me, because I've already been shaken more than most people, and survived. The religion I learned from my adoptive family has had an enormous impact on my life. Even moving across town from my first family to my adoptive family has made a big difference. I met my wife here. I started a business in this area. I choose to live here.

Sometimes I ask myself, "What if I hadn't been adopted?" It's impossible to tell how my life would have turned out—it's like comparing apples to oranges. But I'm very aware of the impact it has had on my life. Being adopted was important. I'm sure it was something that was meant to happen.

I wrote a couple of songs about my adoption experience, which really helped me sort things out for myself. One is about my first night at the Conrads, when I was feeling so confused, but happy to be there.

The second song is called *They Must Have Been Friends*. It imagines the story of my two mothers making a pact in a pre-mortal existence. The song tells of my birth mother having just learned her fate, that she would come to Earth and have eight children and then die young. She knew she would need help. So she shared her fate with a friend, my adoptive mother, and asked her, "I want you to take care of one of my sons. I'll be up here watching, but I trust you to be there for him and to teach him and guide him and give him direction in his life. He's my son, but he's your son, too, if you take on this huge task that I'm asking of you." And my adoptive mother agrees, "Yes, I'll do that for you." And so it happened.

This song came to me one day out of the blue, the words and the music together. I had to pull my truck off the road to write it down. For me, it brought together in a spiritual way all the people and the pieces of my life. It was important that I have both of my mothers in my life. I finally recognized that they were both committed to my welfare, that there was a divine contract between them. Writing this song answered the question in my heart, "Is my adoption part of God's plan for my life? Was this supposed to happen?" And I believe it was.

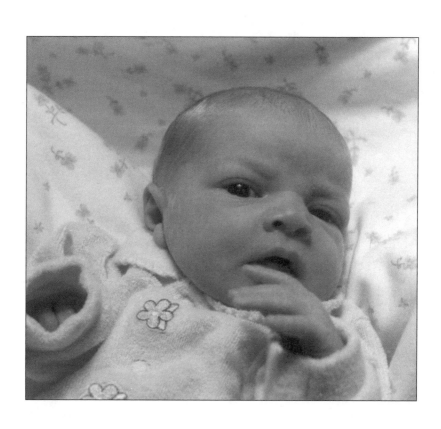

Jennifer

"Adopting Catherine has been a journey of faith. This has been life-changing for me, in more ways than one."

It was Christmas time when we found out that my seventeen-year-old cousin was due to have a baby in early April. In February, we learned that she planned to place the child for adoption. My first reaction was that we should adopt the baby. We had a very comfortable life with three children, a good income, a big house. But my husband has a muscular disease and our youngest child was six, just past the hump of the hard part, so I wrestled with whether we wanted to start over with a baby. I talked to my mom about it and she said, "I don't think you ought to do it, not at this stage of your life." I agreed, "You're right. We should not adopt this baby."

One day soon after, my husband announced, "Jen, I think we ought to adopt Anna's baby." I said, "No, I've already thought it through and decided we shouldn't." I told him my reasoning, he agreed with me, and the idea went away. Or so I thought.

It kept nagging at me. I kept thinking I had already made a decision, but it wouldn't leave me alone. It was still there in the back of my mind in early March, when I went on a women's retreat. I discussed it with some of the women there, one of whom was adopted. I talked to the featured speaker, who was a family counselor, and she told me, "No, don't do it, because you'd just be setting yourself and the child and everybody up for heartache."

That's not what I wanted to hear. I wanted some validation for what I was feeling. I wanted some outside authority to tell me, "Yes, go with your gut." Finally, I went to the chapel there at the retreat, and prayed about it. As I prayed, I realized, "This is not nagging. This is the Lord telling me that this is my path. This is what I need to do. That's why this is not going away for me."

I went home and told my husband and my parents what had happened. Then I picked up the phone and called my uncle, Anna's father, who lived in northern Canada. I told him, "We've been thinking and talking and praying about this, and we want to adopt Anna's baby. How do you feel about that?" He said he'd talk to Anna about it, that it was her decision.

Anna called us the next day and asked two really good questions. First she asked, "Why do you want to adopt my baby? You have three children already." I explained that that was actually one of the reasons we wanted to, because we knew what we'd be getting into. We had a ready-made family to offer this child, a full life. Then she asked, "What took you so long?" So I told her the story about how we had decided, and what a huge decision it was for us to take on another child. I told her we'd only known for a month that she was planning to place the child, so actually, it had been a rather quick decision on our part. And I told her how I felt that the Lord was leading us down this path, that He wanted this child to be with us.

Anna had already chosen an adoptive family for her child, so she said she needed to think about things. She called us back a week later and said, "I want you to adopt my baby."

As soon as she told us that she wanted to place her baby with us, I got on the phone with adoption agencies and lawyers, looking for advice. We live in Georgia, and I learned that if the baby was born in Canada, we could not bring her home until she got a green card, which could take two years. It was not feasible for our whole family to go hang out in Canada for two years. But we certainly didn't want the baby separated from us, so we told Anna, "This will all work out, but you have to come here to have the baby." She agreed to that, so we drove north for two days, while my aunt and uncle and Anna drove south. We met at the border to pick her up and bring her home with us. She was eight-and-a-half months pregnant.

Two weeks later, I was coaching Anna through childbirth, watching our baby being born. I love having babies myself, but this was even more amazing, to watch the baby be born. When I'm the one giving birth, I'm so focused that I miss a lot. So this was very exciting for me. I thought, "Dads are so lucky, to be able to witness this."

My other children and my parents were at the hospital, waiting to meet the newest family member. We didn't know the sex of the baby beforehand, so when my husband and I burst into the waiting room, announcing, "It's a girl!" everyone had to come in and hold her, get their picture taken with her, talk to Anna, cry a little. Then they all went home and I stayed at the hospital with the baby, whom we named Catherine, in the room right next to Anna.

Anna did great! She spent most of the next day with Catherine, getting to know her and saying good-bye. My hat goes off to her, because she was so strong. I cannot imagine birthing a child, then giving it up. I think it helped her to know that this was such an open adoption, and that Catherine was still in the family. I know my aunt and uncle were grateful for that, too. They had a very hard time letting this baby go. What's sweet about the whole thing is that my uncle had been a big part of my life when I was younger. He is my mother's youngest brother, and he was a teenager when I was a baby. He treated me like a favorite pet, more like a little sister than a niece. He would take me to fairs and sing love songs with me. We had not had much contact for years, due to the distance between us. The fact that I now have his granddaughter has brought us back together in a sweet way.

We didn't make a formal agreement with Anna, in terms of visitation or other contact. We did talk about how we thought the relationship ought to be. There won't be any secrets. Catherine will know that she is adopted, and as soon as she is ready to ask, she'll know who her birth parents are. Technically, her relationship to Anna is that of first cousin, once removed. But Anna is also her birth mother. And later, she will know that. She's not even two yet, so at this point, her birth family sends birthday and Christmas gifts and they call every couple of months. The relationship is a long-distance one, because of where we live, so I don't anticipate any big boundary issues.

In the future, I expect Catherine will want to write Anna, phone her, visit occasionally. And because the relationship will already be established, she won't have the trauma of not knowing who she is. I know some adopted kids that don't seem to care who their biological parents are, and others that care a great deal. I don't know much about it, but I assume that the kids who really want to know are the ones who grow up knowing nothing about their heritage. In an open adoption, there's no questioning or wondering. I believe that if you don't hide anything from them, they grow up comfortable and secure with who they are. It's partly a generational thing. Attitudes about adoption have changed. In the old days, there was a lot of secrecy. To me, there seems to be too much shame in that approach, and I know adults who are hurting from it to this day.

Catherine looks so much like my biological kids that we don't get many questions. In a way, that's easier than when your children don't look like you. But even if we tried to hide it, it would come up, because my older kids were part of the whole adoption process. One of the things I love is to watch how my older children enjoy Catherine. They just love her. It's been a great experience for them, to have a baby in the house, someone to love and take care of.

Our relationship with the birth father and his family is different. At first, it was all very messy, because the pregnancy was the result of a one-night stand and he didn't want his parents to find out, so he denied paternity. But Anna was sure it was him. We finally got a lawyer to track him down in Canada, and he admitted that it could be his child. He signed the papers relinquishing his parental rights, so we could go ahead with the adoption. But we've never met him or talked to him.

However, when Catherine was about three months old, I got a phone call from the birth father's mother, who didn't know anything about where the baby had been placed. She didn't know that her granddaughter was in Georgia or that we were related to Anna. We talked for about half an hour and I told her the whole story and why we had adopted her. Then I said, "My only wish is that when Catherine is old enough and wants to know who you all are, that you will have an open door for her. That's all I ask."

She was delighted with that. Since then, they've sent birthday and Christmas cards to Catherine, which I really welcome, because now she'll begin to know who all these people are. She'll understand her story. She'll know why her birth parents gave her up, why she's with us. She'll know she hasn't been deserted. She's just with us to grow up. She needs to know that. When we were deciding to adopt her, it broke my heart to think that if we didn't take her, this child might grow up and wonder, "There are so many people in my birth family. Why didn't somebody want me?" I thought, "We have so much. There is no reason for us not to take this baby. Other than the fact that it's inconvenient to start over with a baby, the blessings are enormous. Look at what we get!" The blessings of having her in our family far outweigh any inconvenience. That's the bottom line for us.

Adopting Catherine has been a journey of faith. I really believe this is the Lord's plan, and I never had faith like this before. This has been huge in my personal life, in terms of my faith. Despite all the legal obstacles, the concerns of my family, and the little glitches along the way, I feel peaceful about the whole thing. I have faith that everything will be fine, because this is the way it's meant to be. This has been life-changing for me, in more ways than one. I'd do it all again in a heartbeat.

 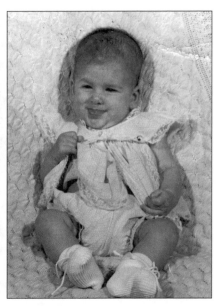

Emerald

"No matter how deep my agony at losing my children, I am nonetheless proud that I did what I set out to do—break the cycle of child abuse in my family."

I have a fantasy of my two children playing together under a summer sky, their dark hair and olive skin glowing. I imagine myself watching them from behind an untended patch of sunflowers. It's their innocence that touches me so deeply. But that's as close to innocence as I'll ever get—and it's only a fantasy.

When I was pregnant with my daughter, I'd study my oddly bulging belly in the mirror. There was a huge void in me, and even though I knew that the purpose of parenthood was not to fill my empty tank, I desperately wanted this baby. Even though I was pregnant by rape, I wanted her. But common sense prevailed. I had a high school education and almost no job skills. I did not want to raise my child on welfare or struggle constantly to balance work and childcare.

Beyond the obvious circumstances, I knew the real reason I ought to place my child elsewhere was a secret I kept safe. I was intimately acquainted with rage. I knew it would threaten and scar my child, the same way I had been wounded by a lifetime of severe abuse. I was determined to end the cycle of child abuse in my family.

So I didn't shop for a car seat or cradle, but for prospective parents. I was apprehensive the day I went to meet Marie and Carl, the first couple on the list from my lawyer. I clutched a long list of questions and debated about how rigid I would be on various issues. When I arrived, I realized they were as nervous as I was. They answered my questions as if they knew what I was looking for, in exact detail. I knew at that very first meeting that I couldn't find a better match, but I didn't want to tell them right away that I wanted them to parent my baby. Timing was important. I wanted it to be memorable.

They drove me home after our day together. As I showed them my humble home, I struggled to know what to say. The air was thick with anticipatory tension. When we entered my bedroom, I saw the two stuffed pandas from my childhood sitting on my bed. One panda was mine and the other was my sister's. She had abandoned hers, and being the maternal little girl that I was, I chose to foster her bear. I left my sister's panda lying on the bed, picked up mine lovingly, and gave it to Marie.

"This is for you," I said. "I kept it on my bed when I was a little girl. I want you to take it now and put it in your crib. You have a baby on the way."

Marie threw her arms around me in thanks. She didn't need to say anything. I already knew something of their heartbreaking struggle to have children. From that moment, I began to see the child within me as a gift I was giving to Marie and Carl, and to view them as a gift I was giving to my baby.

Of course, framing the experience as gift-giving did not miraculously relieve the excruciating pain of giving up my baby. I had no lingering doubts about relinquishing her to them. But I knew it would be desperately hard to let her go. There was a part of me that was almost jealous, because my daughter would have the life I had been deprived of, with parents that would nurture and protect her. I was giving her a chance for a happy childhood. So while I was grieving at losing her, I was also grieving over my own lost innocence. I wanted Marie and Carl to adopt me, too, as if that would erase my history.

My water broke one morning while I was still in bed. I ran to the telephone to call Marie. "Guess what?" I blurted. "I'm headed to the hospital." She didn't know whether to laugh or cry and I was so excited for her that I momentarily forgot about my impending loss. I had never felt so important. I was about to bestow the gift of life. I waited patiently for the contractions to begin, but my body needed a little prodding. Just as I'd concluded that birthing this baby was going to be a walk in the park, things really got moving. My mother was there, and Carole, my social worker, as well as my labor coach, and Marie and Carl. They all had advice for me. I finally yelled, "If I hear my name once more in connection with the word 'breathe,' I'm quitting!"

Carole laughed and asked, "What would you like us to call you?"

"Mud," I replied. I don't remember if they honored my request for the new name, or if they dared tell me to breathe again. The only word I was aching to hear was "Push!" I was afraid I would miss my cue.

My little girl was finally born with a healthy holler. Carl was busy taking pictures of the birth so that someday, their child could see where she came from. After the excitement of the delivery, he leaned against the wall, turned a little green, and started sliding down the wall. I laughed out loud.

When the nurse handed the baby to me, I said, "No, I'm shaking too much to hold her right now. Marie, you hold her first." Marie reached for the baby, tears rolling down her cheeks.

I wanted to take in every detail of this beautiful child, so I snapped mental pictures of everything. I didn't want to ever forget any nuance of her. The next day, I signed the relinquishment papers and said good-bye to my daughter. I held her and fed her and told her all about what her home would be like. I told her about the pets at her house, about the book I had made for her, and about life in general. Sometimes I'd cry so hard my tears would fall on her little face, as if they belonged to her. I talked and cried for about two hours. Then Carl and Marie came to get their daughter.

At that point, I deeply resented them for taking my baby from me. But I was also deeply grateful, and I loved them for adopting my child and giving her the home she deserved. I looked at Carl, whose eyes were red and misty. I felt guilty that I hadn't really made as strong a connection with him as I had with Marie, but I knew that he understood that I had absolutely no experience with safe men. Even though I trusted him, I had little idea of how to communicate with men.

"You be a good father to her," I commanded him. That was all I could say before Marie and I dissolved into tears again. We held our daughter between us, creating a delicate web of mothers' love. Then we walked to the hospital doors together, and I watched the three of them disappear into the dark night. I remained alone.

I dreamt that night, a beautiful dream that gave me comfort and strength to face the long road of grief ahead. I was in a forest and I saw a doe and fawn. I was so entranced by the beauty of the scene that I didn't want to risk even breathing, fearing it would disappear. A song wafted through the forest air and it took some time before I could decipher the words. Finally, I understood. "You did the right thing," soft voices repeated endlessly, like wind in the trees. "You did the right thing."

A year and a half later, I married Jerry, while a few months pregnant with my second child. I did not want to marry him. Part of me despised him, but I was still listening to the tapes in my head that convinced me that no one would marry me anyway, that I was damaged goods. I felt compelled to prove them wrong.

I gave birth to Brandon almost exactly two years after my daughter's birth. When he was three months old, I went back to college. I was overloaded with studying and caring for a baby and Jerry was no help. Our relationship was characterized by emotional and verbal abuse, replicating my earlier life. Finally, I bailed out. I called a women's crisis line and arranged for me and Brandon to go to a shelter.

The two of us began a cycle of instability and shelter hopping, which lasted for two-and-a-half years. We lived in sixteen different places between his birth and his third birthday. As Brandon developed, I started remembering some of my own childhood. Whereas before, there had been large gaps in my memory, horror filled the voids. In therapy, I began having flashbacks of activities at cemeteries and came to realize that what I had experienced as a child was Satanic ritual abuse. I began to notice that I was missing gaps of time in the present and was re-diagnosed with multiple personality disorder. I was hospitalized several times because of cult programming which led me to believe it was my duty to commit suicide.

When Brandon was two-and-a-half years old, we were living in yet another shelter. This shelter required children to be in bed at 8:30, but Brandon was used to staying up later. He was reluctant to go to bed. We shared a room with a mother and her two little children, plus another single woman. I felt extremely pressured to keep my boy quiet, and he was not cooperating one bit. One night, I hit him repeatedly, trying to make him go to sleep. He retaliated by hitting me back. The next thing I knew, I had my hands around his neck, squeezing tight. I was so terrified of getting kicked out of the shelter because of his noise that I resorted to violence. I quickly realized what I was doing and stopped. I started crying and pleaded with Brandon to be quiet so we wouldn't get into trouble. Then I left the room so I wouldn't hurt him anymore.

This was not the first time I had physically mistreated Brandon. It began when he was nine months old and wouldn't sleep through the night. I felt guilty about what I was doing. I went to parenting classes and the problem got worse and better in erratic cycles. By the time my therapists got one pattern figured out and resolved, another would surface. When I found myself with my hands around my son's neck, I knew I had to think seriously about giving up my parental role. Staff members at one shelter had mentioned that most ritual abuse survivors are not able to safely parent. But I couldn't go through the pain of adoption again.

When Brandon turned three, it became clear to me that I was supposed to kill both my child and myself. This was another mental program instilled by the cult. The programming only intensified if I ignored it. I began to have nightmares about being ordered to kill Brandon by dumping him in a grave and shoveling dirt on top of him, burying him alive. In the dream, I couldn't follow through with the orders to kill my son, but I was petrified that I might put the plan into action against my own will. I told my therapist what was happening and she made the decision to put Brandon in foster care. The police came to get him one night, which terrified my poor son, and then he was gone.

Brandon was in foster care three times, each time with the same family. They were very patient and supportive of both of us. Each time I decided I wanted to continue parenting, the death program would resurface. I finally realized it was likely to be recurrent and that it was probably best for Brandon to remove him from the situation permanently.

I remembered when I was pregnant with him, I would rub my stomach and cry in the mornings at the happy thought of keeping this one. I had been in therapy the entire two years between the births of my two children, and I thought I was capable of parenting. But now I knew that for my son's sake, I needed to gather my courage and find him a better life. So I contacted an adoption agency.

Brandon seriously grieved when he arrived at the foster home for the last time. I think he knew that our life together was over. His foster parents held him for days, soothing his pain. I was allowed to visit him whenever I wanted to until the day of his adoption. I told him that his safety was very important to me and that I seemed to have a hard time keeping him safe. I told him he would get a new Mom and Dad, but that he would still get to see me and Jerry. He held onto me, cried a lot, and listened to all that I said. Some days, he appeared to be very mature and took it all matter-of-factly, and other days, he questioned me worriedly about why this had to happen. I reassured and reassured. It was hard to choke back my own tears as his flowed. I did not want my sensitive little boy to feel that he had to take care of me.

I looked through the profiles of people who would be willing to adopt an older child and finally settled on a couple named Lyn and Mark. When I went to meet them at the adoption agency, the air was tense with each party's secret worries. Lyn and Mark had recently experienced a disruption in their adoption of a baby and were still hurting from that. And I was about to lose my second child.

Lyn and Mark spent time with Brandon at the foster home and found him to be as delightful as I knew him to be. But they were slow to decide. I waited a week without hearing anything. It felt like my ego was at stake, that if they chose not to take my child, it was a personal affront. Finally, I called the agency and told them I had changed my mind, that my child was no longer up for adoption.

The counselor replied, "Well, what shall I tell Lyn and Mark? They just called to say they want to adopt Brandon."

I cried, "I don't know! He needs to get settled as soon as possible."

"If I were able to get this moving to completion in a few days, would you do it?" she asked.

I pondered for several minutes while she waited for my answer.

"Yes," I finally blurted. I knew I had to let him go, to give him a life he deserved.

Three days later, Lyn, Mark, and their six-year-old son met with me and Brandon. I held Brandon on my lap, thinking, "Relinquishing a child is just as hard the second time around." Actually, this was harder, because Brandon and I had a history together. Lyn read some scriptures to me, and I read a prayer I had written for the new family. We snapped a few pictures of the whole group, then went downstairs to say good-bye.

When Brandon hugged me good-bye, I broke down sobbing. I was crying so hard that at first he thought I was laughing, and he laughed, too. But when he realized I was crying, he looked worried. He looked me straight in the face, and with wisdom far beyond his three years, he said, "Mom, I am in your heart." I hugged him tight, then let him go.

He got into the car with his new family and I watched until their car disappeared into traffic. I felt completely empty, just like I had when I had watched Marie and Carl walk out of those hospital doors with my daughter five years earlier.

Brandon has been with his new family for over ten years now. That first year was beyond agonizing for me. I attempted suicide, concluding that there was no reason to go on living without either of my children with me. Lyn knew I was struggling and sent me a beautiful card. She let me know that if something were to happen to me, Brandon's foundation would be destroyed. She said he needed me in his life. Every time I felt like giving up, I would remember what she'd said, that Brandon did need me, and that Lyn cared enough about him and about me to let me remain a part of his life. It gradually became a lot more difficult to think about quitting life, until eventually, suicide was the farthest thing from my mind.

Lyn and Mark and I have had a rough road together, developing a relationship that works. We have different views on life, which has led to many heated disagreements and lots of tears. The nature of this adoption led me to view them as profiting from my agony. Only when I shifted my framework could our relationship improve. I realized it wasn't their "fault" that they had Brandon and I didn't. He is a joy in their life, as he is in mine. I finally let go of the feeling that it was a contest over who loved him most. This was an excruciating process of maturation for me, but I am thrilled with the end result. We now have a relationship that is loving, peaceful, and smooth.

I still grieve over relinquishing my two children. But it is easier to accept now, especially since I have been disabled by a neuromuscular disease. I would have been unable to care for them, even physically. I've come to see the whole thing as God's plan. Brandon plants sweet kisses on my cheek when I see him, which I accept as his way of saying "thank you."

I've learned that healing is not a destination—it's a journey. When I was a young teen, I fantasized about saving a child's life. How important I would be then! After the adoptions—after the heavy dust of grief had settled somewhat—I could see that I had saved two children's lives. I was just as important as someone who had run into a burning building and pulled the children to safety. My children are safe. No matter how deep my agony at losing them, I am nonetheless proud that I did what I set out to do—break the cycle of child abuse in my family.

Cathe

"My son's adoption is totally different from mine. It's much more open. It isn't the big secret it was in my home when I was a girl."

I didn't find out I was adopted until I was in sixth grade. I suspected it, because of the way my mom would joke about how the stork dropped me off, or how they found me in a cabbage patch. But I never had anything that spelled it out in black and white, so I wasn't sure. My brother, who is two years older than me, is also adopted, and I found out about both of us at the same time. I was visiting my aunt, who is also my godmother, and she was working on a family tree. She had a list of everybody in the family and next to my name and my brother's name, she had written "adopted."

When I was a little older, I started asking questions. My mom gave me my birth certificate and all my baby pictures and told me what she knew, but the story is still not very clear to me. I know they got me as an infant, but I don't know if they went through an adoption agency, an orphanage, or the Catholic Church.

Adoption is a very private thing for my parents. They feel it's not something that should be discussed or shared. I got the sense they were somehow ashamed of it. Maybe it had something to do with the fact that they couldn't have children biologically. But being adopted doesn't bother me at all. I don't think it's a big deal, so it's hard for me to understand their attitude. If anyone should be upset, it seems like it should be me, but I'm perfectly fine with it.

I always knew my parents loved me, even though they weren't very affectionate. They always encouraged my brother and me to be self-sufficient, and though we certainly weren't spoiled brats, I had everything I could want. My parents were good planners and good providers. But I don't feel very close to them, even though we get along fine.

My brother found his birth mother recently, and though she chooses not to meet him at this point, he did meet his biological sister and brother. He asked me if I wanted to find my birth parents, and I told him, "I can't. I've tried." My birth certificate lists only the last name of my birth mother, which is not very helpful in trying to track someone on the Internet.

I don't have a great desire to find my birth parents, anyway. The only reason I searched at all was to see if I could find out if I have any siblings. It would be nice to know if there is anything of concern in my birth family's health history, as well. And it might be interesting to see who I resemble, but other than that, I figure it's a done deal and better left alone. I'm sure my birth mother did what she did for a reason. I wouldn't want to bring up any bad memories for her, because I don't know what she went through or why she had to give me up. I never play "What if?" about my life, or imagine different scenarios.

My son's adoption is totally different. It's much more open. My husband and I were looking forward to having kids, but we found out after several years of trying that I can't have children. So we decided to adopt.

We chose an adoption agency, wrote short autobiographies, collected pictures, and went through several interviews. The agency collected all this information from us to make available to birth parents who come to the agency to place a child. Then we waited. We waited almost two years before we got Jacob.

We had a fortunate situation because we had both a birth mother and a birth father involved. We were living in Utah at the time and the birth parents were from the South. They were an unmarried couple with two children already. The birth mother was twenty and the birth father nineteen, so they were both young and feeling overwhelmed. They decided to adopt this child out, because they didn't feel like they could take care of one more. Neither one of them had a job, they had no place to live, and her mother was supporting them. What's nice about the agency we used is that they try to help birth parents get back on their feet. They brought the couple to Utah for the last couple of months of the pregnancy and set them up in an apartment, made sure the birth mother got medical care and good food, and basically took care of them.

We met the birth parents at the agency and they told us their story—where they are from, how they wound up in this situation, why they were placing this child. Later, we took them to dinner and helped them move into their apartment. We spent a lot of time together over the next few weeks. My husband and the birth father have a lot in common, so they really enjoyed each other. Both birth parents are great kids. They're just young and naive and don't really have their life together yet.

At their invitation, we were at the birth, which was an amazing experience. After Jacob was born, he had to stay in the hospital overnight. They let the birth father stay, too, and their youngest son, but the hospital wouldn't let their four-year-old stay, so we took him home to spend the night with us. He was so sweet, I thought, "Gee, I'll take this one!"

As it turned out, Jacob stayed in the hospital for almost two weeks, because they thought he might have strep. It was so sad to see my tiny little son hooked up to a bunch of machines. I just wanted to scoop him up and take him home. We visited him every night, even though we lived an hour-and-a-half away.

This was supposed to be a semi-open adoption, with the agency acting as mediator, but it's turned out a little differently. I had a long chat with the birth mother in the hospital, and it seemed clear that she just wanted to be done with it, so I didn't push anything. I told them both, "I'm more than willing to do pictures, letters, and phone calls, but I'm not good at initiating that sort of thing, so if you want it, just ask."

That first year, we took pictures, wrote letters, and made a video for the birth parents. Then we sent it all to the agency, so they could get it to them. But I don't know if they ever got anything. The birth parents did call us occasionally, through the agency, but we haven't heard from them in quite a while. I think they went back home, but I'm not sure exactly where they are.

My parents were supportive of our adoption, though they never knew how much contact we had with the birth parents. My dad told me, "I always knew you'd be a good mom," and that's nice to hear. My husband's parents are like kid magnets, the perfect picture of Grandma and Grandpa. This will be our only child, so Jacob is spoiled rotten.

Jacob is still too young to understand his story. We have a children's book on adoption that we read to him all the time, so I don't think he'll have a hard time understanding it. He hears us talk about it, but it's not something we sit down and discuss with him yet. He's only four. But it certainly isn't the secret it was in my home when I was a girl.

I think everyone should adopt, if they have the desire, the ability, and the money. But you shouldn't adopt just to make yourself feel noble, or to look good. If you really want to do it, and you know what you're getting into, it's a great thing.

I'm very grateful to my birth mother for doing what she felt she had to do. That is a tremendous decision for anyone to have to make. I have the utmost respect for birth parents, for anyone who can say, "I cannot raise this child properly, so I need to give it to someone who can." That's so much better than trying to do it yourself, then failing the child in some major way. It takes an enormous amount of courage and trust. And I certainly appreciate that, both as a daughter and a mother.

Wayne

*"In my mind, my mother and father were my mother and
father, and I had no curiosity about my original parents."*

I don't know why I was put up for adoption. I've never known any
mother or father other than my adoptive parents. And they didn't
tell me much. I don't think they knew much. People didn't talk
about these things in those days.

I was born in 1928 and I'm sure I came home to my adoptive
family as a newborn. I don't even know if I was born in a hospital or
not, but I presume the doctor that handled the birth arranged for my
adoption. That's how it was typically done then.

I bet my natural parents had no idea where I went. I just believe
that—that they didn't have a clue. I think the doctor took me as soon
as I could be separated from my birth mother and handed me over to
my parents. That's the way I figure it happened.

I do remember the day my mother told me I was adopted. I must
have been about five years old, and I remember lying beside her on her
bed. She explained what a natural, biological birth was and how I
came to be. Then she told me that she and my father had adopted me

when I was a baby. She didn't explain from whom I came or who my biological father was. So I have no clue about that.

I've never had any real interest in looking up my birth parents. I have a registration of birth, which identifies me as the son of my adoptive parents. It's not the same thing as a birth certificate. I suppose if I wanted to find out who my biological parents were, I could go to the State of Pennsylvania and request to see my birth certificate. But I've never done that. In my mind, my mother and father were my mother and father, and I had no curiosity about my original parents. I didn't wonder who I looked like, or what my natural parents did, or why they didn't keep me. I'm just not curious about it.

Other than the time my mother told me I was adopted, we didn't talk about adoption in the family. My brother, Dick, who is three years older than I am, was also adopted. But I never knew anything about how my parents got him. It just wasn't discussed. I don't know why. Lots of things weren't discussed at that time. I didn't know of any other kids in our town who were adopted. It seems like adoption became a big deal after World War II. Before then, nobody ever talked about it. Dick and I didn't talk about it. We were just family, as far as I was concerned. As for being adopted or not, I don't think it's made one iota of difference in either my life or Dick's.

Dick and I got along all right. We were complete opposites. I was a goody-goody guy and Dick really caused a lot of problems. I could see the pain that he was causing my folks and maybe that's why I was no problem at all. No doubt about it, I was a model child. I didn't want to give my mother and dad the grief that Dick gave them. He was just one of those kids. I don't know if it was his genes or something else that made him such a rabble-rouser. There's always been a big controversy over what's more important—environment or heredity. And I don't know the answer to that.

Around 1940, our whole family went down to the county courthouse and Dick and I went through a legal adoption procedure in front of a judge. I don't know what documentation our parents had to show we were adopted, and I assume they took this further legal step for inheritance purposes. I testified before the judge and it was all recorded. My parents had prepped me before we went. They told me what we were going to do. It didn't feel like a big deal to me, since my parents were already my parents.

I never had any issues related to being adopted. I often wonder where I'd be if I hadn't been adopted, but with a sense of gratitude, rather than regret. I just think, "Thank God I'm in the family I am." I never ask, "Would I be better off somewhere else?" It's just curiosity, to wonder, "What would I be doing now if I hadn't been adopted by these two people?" But it's never gotten to the point where I want to search out my birth family. I feel very connected to my family, very content.

I've seen the adoption scene change over the years. It's become much more open. It makes me wonder about the emotional impact on the children. I had no emotional connection to anyone other than my adoptive family, and I think that's good. So I wonder about open adoption, where the adopting parents and the natural parents know each other and they agree that the child is going to know both, growing up. I just wonder how that's going to work out. I don't have an opinion about it, but I'm interested to see how those arrangements will work out. I don't know any adults who have been adopted under those circumstances, so it's hard to know. I'm sure there are a lot of open adoptions now—I know of several personally—but it's a fairly new trend in adoption, at least in my lifetime. I'm probably not going to see how it all turns out, because I'm not going to live that long. But I can wonder.

Leslie

"She told me, 'I did some research and it looks like there are a lot of lesbians with children and the kids seem to do just fine.'"

I have always wanted a child. When I was twelve years old, my parents asked me what I wanted for my birthday, and I said, "I want a baby." So they bought me a baby doll, but it wasn't the same. I always dreamed of growing up and having seven kids. I had names all picked out. I really wanted to be a mommy.

It's a little trickier to be a mommy when you're a lesbian. I didn't want to parent by myself, although I had reached the point where I was considering it. I have had relationships break up over this issue. So when I met my partner, one of the first things I said was, "I want kids." She was ambivalent at first, but after a lot of discussion, we decided to try to have a baby.

I wanted to experience pregnancy, too, partly because my mom and my sister both loved the experience. So my partner and I decided that I would be the one to carry the child. We joined a "Baby Maybe" group at a local Lesbian Resource Center, out of which we formed a smaller support group of four couples.

My partner and I tried insemination about twenty times, first at home, then using medical intervention. We tried fertility drugs, intra-uterine insemination, a change in doctors, more drugs. I never became pregnant, so my partner tried a few times, but with no better result.

The infertility issue was a mixed thing for me. There was no way any child we had would be related to both of us, so adoption was always going to be involved. One of us would be adopting a child that was not biologically related. But I still had a deep desire to be pregnant, not necessarily so that my child would be biologically related to me, but just for the experience. I still wonder what that would be like. It's not a huge grief, but it is a loss.

It was frustrating, because during that time period, the other three couples in our support group all had children, either by birth or adoption. We also had three nieces and nephews born during that time. My partner and I were at my cousin's wedding, in the midst of all our trying, and part of their vows included a promise to "be the mother (or father) of your children." We sat there muttering to each other, "It's not that easy, you know. You can't just go and get pregnant." Of course, they got pregnant on the first try, and have a beautiful child now.

It seemed like everyone around us was having babies and we were having this infertility crisis. Getting pregnant becomes a quest. You want to have children and then when you can't, you forget about actually having the children, and you get caught up in how to get pregnant. We thought about that, at this point. We started asking ourselves, "Do we really want a child? Do we even have any idea what it will be like to be parents?" The infertility experience actually helped us clarify what we really wanted.

What we really wanted was a child. So we started the adoption process. We had looked at adoption before, but when it became clear that we could either throw our money at a very slim chance of conception, or put our money toward adoption, we decided, "Let's adopt."

Initially, we considered adopting from China, but the paperwork and the expense were daunting, not to mention how much we would have to hide about ourselves. So we looked into domestic agencies that were open to adopting to lesbian couples. We started with an agency on the East Coast that we found on the Internet, but after several months of runaround, I began to get uneasy about it. The whole thing felt phony to me, so we backed out.

We first heard about open adoption at a basketball game from two women with a baby who were sitting in front of us. They told us about the open adoption agency they had used, so we contacted the agency and got some information. We then went through the whole process of figuring out what open adoption meant. We started reading books for information and experiences. We read one open adoption story in which the birth parents chose the baby's name. That shook us up, because names are very important to us, and we thought that if we didn't get to name the baby, we probably couldn't go this route. But when we started talking to people who were already involved in open adoptions, we realized that this is not generally the case. We began to feel much better about it, much more comfortable. We finally decided, "We can do this. This is not anything too weird." So we went to the orientation meeting at the agency and began the process.

We waited a year, after completing our home study and all the paperwork. Nothing happened. We were beginning to lose hope, so we thought we ought to start pursuing adoption through the State, as well, in case a foster adoption came up first. The first step in adopting through the State of Washington is to take several classes. So my partner was at an AIDS awareness class the Saturday morning that we got The Call. I was at our house, which was a big mess, because we had just re-floored the kitchen. The refrigerator was in the living room, the back bedroom was jammed with all our kitchen stuff, and I was sewing stockings for my nieces and nephews. And that's when the agency called and announced, "You've been chosen."

Ben had been born the night before to a woman who didn't even know she was pregnant. He was a surprise to everybody. The birth mother has a very close family, and her mother, her aunt and a couple of cousins were all there at the hospital with her. The birth father was also there, and they all talked about whether they could raise this child or not. Together, they decided that it would be better to place the baby with an adoptive family.

The hospital suggested some adoption agencies, and the family liked the idea of open adoption, so our agency sent a social worker over to meet with them. She brought with her three identical books full of letters from prospective parents. Ben's grandmother was looking through one book, his aunt was looking through another, and his birth parents were searching the third. Ben's aunt and his grandmother didn't want to tell the birth parents who they liked, because they didn't want to influence their decision. But they all picked us, independent of each other. Later, they said they chose us because it seemed like we would be very open and they really wanted to have this child in their life and because we have a lot of animals and they are animal lovers. Also, the birth father noted that my partner is Jewish and our letter said we would raise our child Jewish, and he really wanted that.

As soon as the agency called, I got ahold of my partner, and we went to the hospital to meet with the birth family and the social workers. There were about fourteen of us packed into a little room, all for this little baby. We chatted about it, but it was odd, because no one asked us if we wanted to adopt him, and we didn't know if we were supposed to say, "We'll take him." My partner and I finally stepped out of the room with the agency social worker and asked her, "Should we ask them if we can adopt him, or what?" She went and talked to the family for a few minutes, then came back and told us, "They were afraid you wouldn't want him." After everyone was clear that the family wanted us and we wanted Ben, we were sent home with instructions to come back the next day for an infant care class and to take Ben home.

We spent the rest of the evening getting ready for a baby. We shopped for diapers, formula, and gifts for the birth parents. We cleaned out the back bedroom and set up a crib. Then I paced the whole night through, since I couldn't sleep.

When we went back to the hospital the next morning, Ben's aunt asked, "Did you get any sleep?"

"No!" I said.

She laughed and said, "We did. I struggled with whether we really wanted to go through with this, and I did some research on the Internet about children of lesbians. It looks like there are a lot of lesbians with children and the kids seem to do just fine. So I'm feeling much more calm and sure about this."

We didn't do anything ceremonious when we took our son home. After the infant care class, we went into the room where Ben was waiting with his birth family, to get our baby and to say goodbye. It was hard, because everything had happened so fast—for everybody. We promised to love him and take care of him. Everybody cried. Then they left, and we put Ben in his new car seat, put him in the car, and drove home. We carried the car seat in and set it on the table. We stared at the baby, then at each other, and said, "What have we done?" It was Sunday afternoon. This had all happened in a weekend. I called my boss and announced, "I'm a mom. I won't be in to work tomorrow."

Those first few months were really tough, trying to juggle work and parenthood. After two weeks off, I went back to work part-time, which just meant I was doing all the work in half the time. Then I'd rush home, so my partner could get her work done. It was stressful, and I got very sick. Finally, my partner closed down her business to stay home full-time with Ben, while I moved to a larger firm and went back to working full-time. That was actually easier than the tag-team parenting we had been doing.

The exhaustion is something no one can explain to you. People told me, "Oh, you'll be tired." But there's no way to prepare for something that comes up when you're totally exhausted, when you have to just dig deep and say, "Okay, I'm the adult here." Everything may be falling apart and you want to fall apart, too, but you can't. Parenting is so much harder, in some ways, than anybody ever tells you, but it's also so much more amazing. To be a parent is to pull from the deepest roots you have. You really find out who you are.

Ben's birth family is very involved in his life. Our contract says they get six visits a year, but we see them more than that. The birth mother's family is large and very cohesive. Ben is the first child of the next generation in their family, and I know there is still a great sadness about him sometimes. They had no time to prepare for this. He surprised the world. I don't sense any regret on their part for placing him with us, just a normal grief.

Open adoption is like having in-laws. That's neither good nor bad, but it creates more logistical challenges. You have more family to deal with. But I like our relationship with the birth family. They're a good group of people. We went into these relationships totally for Ben's sake, but they have really enriched our own lives. His birth family is very caring and it's nice to be part of their family and have them be part of ours. I remember the day they called to invite us to their Fourth of July picnic. Ben's birth grandmother said, "Well, you're family now, so bring something." That felt good.

Ben is almost five years old now and he still has a very open relationship with his birth family. He spends the weekend with them several times a year, as well as occasional days. It is a rich and important relationship in his life and in ours.

I've been surprised at how supportive society in general has been toward our little family. I was worried about it, but the risk has been worth it. Most people, after some initial discomfort here and there, are very accepting. We find little gifts of support in unexpected places. The people I work with, for instance, are very supportive. We make sure Ben has places where he is happy and comfortable with having two moms. He knows other kids with the same kind of family, which will give him support and strength to deal with whatever comes up. And there are older kids already burning that path for him. So it's less of an issue than it used to be, especially where we live.

We also make sure he has good male role models in his life. My brother is quite enthused about being Ben's uncle and Ben gets a lot from that relationship. There are also some great men in his birth family, so that is a resource, too. I want to make sure he has guys he can talk to, that will be there for him. I think there is some level of communication and understanding between men that doesn't come out verbally. I can't even begin to know what that's all about—it's some culture all their own. And I want Ben to experience that.

Ben is now a big brother. His little brother joined our family when he was five days old as a foster child, and we expect this second adoption to be finalized within a few months. Even though I've always dreamed of being a mom, the journey is so much more amazing than I could have ever imagined. Parenting is the biggest adventure of my life. It's my dream come true.

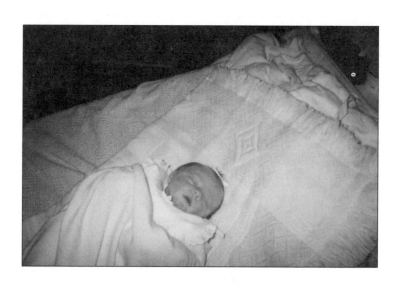

Carolyn

"I shared with my daughter the unwelcome, yet sweet impression that had come to me about gifting her baby to someone else."

I came home from work one Friday afternoon in July to find that my grown daughter, Kasey, had come to visit from out of state unannounced. Normally, none of my three grown children surprise me like that, so it struck me as odd.

"What are you doing here?" I asked.

"Oh, I just came to surprise you," she said. It fleetingly crossed my mind that she sounded nervous.

"Well, you succeeded!"

We went about preparing dinner and I could feel that something was going on. After dinner, Kasey and her younger sister, Brynn, who still lived at home with me and her stepfather, were cleaning up the kitchen.

After a lengthy silence, Kasey said uneasily, "Mom, we need to go for a walk. We need to talk."

I saw Brynn glance quickly at Kasey, and I knew something big was up.

With a sense of foreboding, I went to my bedroom to put on my tennis shoes. Although I had no idea what she needed to discuss, the sense of urgency in the air gave me a chill. What could it be? What did she need to tell me? Of my four children, Kasey had always been the one to bring bad news, no matter who it pertained to.

I walked out the front door, Kasey right by my side. I said, "Kasey, tell me right now what is going on."

She said, "I can't. I think I'm going to throw up."

"I'm the one that's going to throw up if you don't tell me," I said.

We walked down the driveway toward the street in silence. The tension was killing me.

Suddenly, she blurted, "Brynn's pregnant."

"What?!" I exclaimed, dumbfounded. "Who's the father?" Brynn had just graduated from high school and she had a boyfriend who had been away for about a year, so I knew it wasn't him. I couldn't think who it might be.

"Ben's the father," Kasey said.

I have never been so stunned in all my life. It was like an out-of-body experience. My knees buckled and I sank to the pavement, muttering, "Oh no! Oh my gosh!"

Finally, I got up off the ground and started walking as fast as I could around a three-mile circle in our neighborhood, Kasey trotting beside me. I don't remember what we said to each other. I don't remember what I thought or felt. I was absolutely stunned. Ben was a casual friend of Brynn's, or so I had thought.

When we got back to the house, I went downstairs and found Brynn curled up on the couch. "What are we going to do?" I croaked. Then I grabbed her, hugged her tight and tried to sound reassuring as I whispered, "We'll get through this." She started to cry. I didn't sleep that night.

The next evening, we had company for dinner. I was in such a daze, I don't know how I managed it. Brynn and Kasey were helping me with dinner and every time I looked at Brynn, I saw her with new eyes. She looked all grown-up. Even one of our guests commented on how mature she had become. She's my baby, but she had a different aura about her. It was almost eerie.

I didn't mention Brynn's pregnancy to my husband for about a month. We have a roller-coaster relationship and I was wary of his reaction. He and my children had never formed a family bond, and I certainly didn't want him to make life any more difficult for Brynn by getting angry. But it got to the point where I was physically, emotionally, and mentally sick with worrying over it. I was constantly snapping at him. I finally realized, "I've got to stop this. It's not fair, because he doesn't know what's going on." So one evening, I abruptly announced, "I have to tell you something." Then I took a big breath and blurted, "Brynn's pregnant."

He immediately started yelling at me. It was terrible. I can't remember what he thought she should do. He didn't propose to kick her out during the pregnancy, but he made it clear that if she kept the baby, they could not stay in his house, under his roof.

I was devastated. From that point on, I never discussed with him what I was feeling or how Brynn was doing, which was very hard. I felt very alone. I felt like I had no one to lean on, no shoulder to cry on, no one to provide comfort. I didn't even tell my co-workers until the day Brynn had the baby. I did talk to my other children, because they knew what was happening, and they were very supportive of Brynn. This baby was part of our family, but none of us knew what would happen.

I knew I needed help to cope with this, and for me, prayer became my refuge. Praying had never been an easy thing for me. I had struggled to find my spiritual niche and had typically resorted to prayer only in dire circumstances, when I was desperate. Well, I was desperate now, but I was also very humble and sincere in my need for guidance. I had nowhere else to go, no one else to turn to. I needed to be given direction, so I could help direct Brynn. So I prayed a lot. That's how I survived.

I keenly felt that as Brynn's mother, it was my obligation to share with her whatever was revealed to me through the power of prayer. I didn't know what she should do, what would be the best thing. I knew it wasn't my decision. It was Brynn's decision, and I wasn't going to issue edicts. But I did feel the responsibility to guide her, to tell her of any spiritual impressions that came in answer to my prayers. I don't know if it came across that way to Brynn, but that's what I tried to do as her mother.

I remember thinking how easy an abortion would be. Life could just go on as it had. Philosophically, I'm against abortion, but I could understand why people, at a desperate time, might choose that option. I had always flippantly told my children, "If you ever get pregnant outside of marriage, you'll put that baby up for adoption, and that's that." Of course, I never thought I'd find myself in a position that required such a decision. Now that it was staring me in the face, I discovered that it's not a cut and dried issue. When I hear people spout off that adoption is the only solution, I think, "You have no idea. You have no idea how hard that choice is."

Brynn was four months pregnant and nothing had crystalized. She was still floundering about what to do. One night, I couldn't sleep, so I prayed and prayed, pleading for help, and finally dozed off about two o' clock in the morning. I woke up suddenly a short time later and found myself thinking, "She won't be giving up the baby. She'll be gifting the baby." I knew it was an answer to my prayer, because it felt so profound to me, and I've never considered myself a profound person. But it was not the answer I wanted and I started to cry. I wanted Brynn to somehow be able to keep the baby. We knew by this time that it was a little girl—my granddaughter. Gifting her just couldn't be the right answer. I would have to keep praying.

I didn't tell Brynn about that night for quite some time. She's very private and keeps things close to herself, so I knew I had to weigh my words carefully. In the meantime, I kept praying, hoping for a different answer. Then one day Brynn came to my workplace and we went for a walk. As we were puffing and panting up a nearby hill, I was suddenly prompted to tell her what had happened. I said, "Brynn, I need to tell you something and I want you to just listen. Please don't think I'm trying to force anything on you, but I have to tell you what happened to me." Then I shared with her the unwelcome, yet sweet impression that had come to me about gifting her baby to someone else. She listened, but did not respond.

Meanwhile, Ben had left for college out of state. He had made some attempts to be involved, but Brynn did not want him in the picture. He told her, "Whatever you decide, I'll support." Then he was gone.

Brynn's boyfriend, Micah, came home in November. She had written him about her pregnancy just before his return. Everyone had long presumed that Micah and Brynn would eventually marry and live happily ever after. Needless to say, when we met Micah at the airport, it was very awkward. There was such a sadness in the air. There were no good answers to the questions, "Why? How did this happen? Why?"

Micah told Brynn he would be supportive of her through her pregnancy, and he was. Brynn was very close to Micah's family, especially his mother, and she spent a lot of time at their house. I wish it could have been different. I wish I had been with her more, that my home could have been her refuge. Unfortunately, I had not found a way to buffer my children from my husband, so I rationalized that it was good that she had a place to go that insulated her from her stepfather.

I found out much later that my husband had confronted Brynn and made it clear that once the baby was born, she was to make arrangements to be out of his house. He told her that she had made an adult decision and that she had to carry on as an adult. Then he backed off, and to my knowledge, never said another word to her about the baby. Brynn avoided him as best she could. She was going to school full-time and working, and she spent most of her extra time at Micah's house.

Christmas came. At that point, Brynn had decided to keep the baby. She called her Bree and began buying baby supplies. I was trying to adjust myself to her plan, although I didn't see how it was going to work. I just embraced Scarlett O'Hara's attitude and told myself, "Oh well, we'll figure it all out tomorrow."

I also kept remembering the gifting impression that I'd had, and though I kept praying, I never felt anything different. I still felt that Bree was supposed to go to another family, even though I didn't want her to and even though Brynn had not chosen that path. I was massively confused about everything. I'd always been of the mind that if something is right, even though it's difficult, things will fall into place. But things were not falling into place. Instead, it was nettlesome, like strings hanging in my eyes that I couldn't brush away. I kept thinking, "We'll work it out. If this is what she chooses to do, we'll work it out somehow." But the way never became clear.

In January, I awoke from a deep sleep one night with the scripture from Ecclesiastes running through my head, the one about there being a time and a season for every purpose. And the thought resounded in my mind, "It's not her time. It's not Brynn's season to be a mother." Again, it was such a profound feeling. I just lay there and let it wash over me.

I still felt an obligation as her mother to share these things with Brynn, these thoughts and impressions that clearly were not coming from me. So I looked for an opportunity to tell her, knowing it might upset her.

That opportunity didn't come until near the end of February. The baby was due in a month. I was at work when I received an e-mail from my oldest daughter, Chris. She, too, had been praying, and felt, like I did, that this wasn't the time for Brynn to be a mother. She wrote, "Mom, we should be helping Brynn plan her baby's room, but instead, we don't even know where the room is." I just started bawling.

That evening, I approached Brynn and said, "I received an e-mail from Chris today that I'd like you to read. I also need to tell you about an experience I had recently." At this point, Brynn was very defensive about keeping the baby. So when I showed her the e-mail and told her about the Ecclesiastes experience, she got very angry. Was I overstepping my bounds? I don't know, but I honestly felt that as her mother, I had to tell her what I was feeling, that I wouldn't be doing my part if I didn't.

I told her, "Brynn, I can't deny the impressions I'm receiving. They happened. Believe me, this is not the answer I want. I want you to be able to keep this baby. I wish I could see a way, but it is so mired in confusion that I don't know how it could be the right thing to do. Bree deserves a Mom and a Dad. And when I think about you adopting her out, I get a weird kind of peace. You take it for what it's worth. Please think about what I'm saying and I'll come back later and we'll talk."

I came back to her room late that night and found her in bed, filling out the adoption papers that she had had for months. She looked at me and said, "Mom, help me." So I crawled into bed with her and we filled out the papers. She turned them into the agency the next day.

Brynn invited me to come with her to the agency to look through the profiles of prospective parents. Her caseworker—a wonderful, soft-spoken woman—explained to Brynn right up front that adoption was not always the answer. Then she gently led my daughter to know her own heart, to discover what was right for herself and her baby. The caseworker looked over Brynn's papers and gave her five biographies to consider. Brynn carefully pored over each file, and eventually chose Noah and Allie.

On March 1st, Brynn and I went to the agency to meet Noah and Allie. They had been married eight years and were aching to have a child. Allie is bigger than Brynn, but has similar facial features, while Noah is very sweet and has a mischievous sparkle about him. Brynn felt an immediate connection with them, and when we left, both of us were smiling. Brynn said, "This is good."

Six days later, I woke up with Brynn on my mind and decided, "I'm not going to work today. I'm going to spend the day with Brynn." We have a small courtyard in front of our house and we spent the entire day planting it with flowers. Throughout her pregnancy, Brynn had referred to Bree as her "Angel Baby" and after we'd finished, I said, "This is going to be our 'Angel Baby Garden,' a place to honor Bree." That little garden has become very special to me.

The next day, I went to work and kept getting interrupted by calls from Brynn. "Mom, I'm having these really funny feelings." It was two weeks before her due date, but I told her, "Start watching the clock and see if there's a pattern to your funny feelings." So she did, and we soon concluded she was in labor.

I was very proud of the way Brynn brought her Angel Baby into the world. She gave birth to her with a sense of modesty and dignity that belied her young age. Micah spent the entire day by her side, and when Bree was born that evening, he broke down crying. My own heart was breaking—for all of us.

Bree was a perfectly darling, beautiful little baby. I looked at her and felt an immediate, overwhelming love. In that moment, she was Brynn's baby—my granddaughter—but I thought, "I can't allow myself to bond with her. It will be too painful to let her go."

Bree was born late in the day on a Wednesday and Utah State law mandates a twenty-four hour waiting period before a birth mother can relinquish her baby. Because that would have made it too late in the day on Thursday, ours was scheduled for Friday morning. That was almost too much time for Brynn. She kept Bree with her the entire time and a deep bond was formed during that short period of time. It was hard to watch them together, knowing that the end was fast approaching.

Brynn's sisters had come to be with her for the birth and to support her through the relinquishment. I had gone home Thursday night to sleep, but Chris and Kasey stayed at the hospital. At four o' clock in the morning, I received a frantic call from Kasey. "Mom, you've got to get over here. You've got to help Brynn."

When I arrived at the hospital, the feeling in the room was frenzied. Brynn was near hysteria. She hadn't slept all night and her eyes were glazed. She was holding on to Bree for dear life. My heart was breaking, but I told her, "Honey, you've made a decision. You know in your heart what you are supposed to do." I realized that I wasn't providing any comfort, so I finally told her that I was going home to get cleaned up and that I would be back about nine o' clock. When I got in my car, I was wracked with grief. I cried all the way home, pleading with God, "Help her. Please send her an angel. This is beyond me. I have done everything I can do."

When I returned to the hospital, things felt calmer, but there was still an edge in the air. A nurse slipped quietly into the room and started talking softly to Brynn, sitting on her bed and gently stroking her hair. The effect of her kindness was palpable—I could feel the air in the room getting lighter. She told Brynn that she had adopted four children and that she thinks of their birth mothers every day and wishes she could personally thank them for the gift of her children. I sat in the corner, watching and listening, and it suddenly dawned on me, "Oh my gosh, you're the angel I prayed for."

I left the room to give the nurse some private time with Brynn, and when I returned, I found Brynn dressing Bree. She had decided to give her to Noah and Allie at the agency office instead of at the hospital, so she was getting her ready. Brynn had bought her a little white outfit and Bree truly looked like an Angel Baby.

I drove Brynn and Bree from the hospital to the agency office. That was the longest, most heart-wrenching five miles I will ever travel. I felt like I was transporting my precious daughter down the green mile, that long trek to the executioner's chair. When we arrived, I noticed two vans full of obviously happy people in the front parking lot. Later, we learned they were members of Noah's and Allie's extended family, come to welcome this new child into their family.

We parked in the back and entered the building through an inconspicuous side door. We were escorted into a private room, where Brynn was told she could take her time saying good-bye to Bree. I took a lot of pictures, trying to capture those bittersweet moments. I keep those pictures tucked away, because I still can't bear to look at them.

When Brynn finally took Bree to Noah and Allie, I remained behind, sitting in the rocking chair that had just held my daughter and granddaughter. Brynn came back alone and we walked out the side door together. Bree was gone.

That first year, I cried all the time. I'd be driving down the street and suddenly be consumed with a sadness that defies description, a pain deeper than I have ever known. It was the biggest sense of loss I have experienced in my life. The only way I could survive the pain during this time was to tell myself we'd simply loaned Bree out for a while, but that she would be returned to us. I'm past that kind of thinking, but for a year or so, that was the salve I used to soothe my broken heart.

In my head, I know that adoption was the right thing to do for Bree, but my heart isn't always convinced, because it remains a very painful experience. There really isn't a perfect "right thing" in these situations. Yes, it was the right thing, but it was a horrible right thing. I've gained a lot more empathy for people in similar circumstances. I'm amazed at how many people have some experience with adoption, from one end or the other. And I bristle when someone takes a hard-line stance about it, as if it's a black and white issue. It's not a simple decision. The "right thing" isn't always crystal clear, and it's certainly never easy. There are a lot of different ways to be "right."

As time passes, the sadness grows more sweet than bitter. I still have days when the loss overwhelms me. When that happens, I just die for Brynn. If this is how I feel, what must she be feeling? She paid the ultimate price to do the right thing. She's my hero. And now that she and Micah are married and have a daughter of their own, now that life has come full circle, I'm beginning to see the fruits of that sacrifice.

Brynn received letters and pictures from Allie and Noah for the first few years, but this is basically a closed adoption, so she no longer has any contact. But the transition time allowed Brynn to find a comfort zone with the separation.

I do have hopes for a future relationship. The agency opens the records when Bree turns eighteen. Someday, I want Bree to know first-hand that she was gifted because she was so loved. I want her to know that there are a lot of people that she's never known that have nonetheless thought about her, cared about her, wondered about her, missed her, prayed for her, and loved her deeply every single day of her life.

Just before Bree's first birthday, Brynn said to me, "Mom, I want to do what I would have done if Bree were with us for her special day. Let's celebrate." So we spent the day at the zoo with Chris and her young son, had lunch at a little café, and visited a delightful children's shop, where we each bought a small gift for Bree. It was a perfect day—a wonderful tribute to a birth mother and the daughter she loved enough to gift to someone else.

I hope someday I'll get to tell Bree about some of the things that happened at the beginning of her life. I'd like to tell her face to face that she will always be our Angel Baby.

Ann

"There's no way to honestly make any general remarks about the difference between raising biological children and adopted children. So much depends on the child."

In 1969, overpopulation was the issue of the day. My husband and I had three healthy boys and we felt guilty even thinking about having another biological child, so we decided to adopt our fourth child. And why not a guaranteed girl, since we had a choice?

When we called the State adoption agency, they told us, "Sure, there are loads of children available for adoption." But by the time we got our paperwork completed, the adoption scene had changed. Up until then, birth control had actually been illegal in Massachusetts, but when it became readily available, there were consequently far fewer children available for adoption. We waited two years for a child, which was very frustrating. Every so often, the agency would call and ask if we would be interested in a non-white child. We always responded, "Yes! Do you have a child for us?" The social worker invariably said, "Maybe in a couple of weeks." But nothing ever came through.

Finally, we called an agency that did international adoptions and were told that we could get a child from Korea fairly quickly. We had known about this option all along, and wished we had pursued it two years earlier. We were so tired of waiting, not knowing where our daughter was. We just wanted to find her and bring her home.

The international agency used our original home study report, but also required some additional information. Their questionnaire asked us to prove that we could afford another child, so I went to our bank for advice on how to prove our financial worthiness. The teller suggested, "Why don't I photocopy your savings passbook?" We sent the agency the photocopy, showing we had $770 in savings, which apparently was proof enough that we could afford a fourth child.

We also had to talk with another social worker. This one was young—perhaps twenty-two years old—and expecting her first baby. It seemed ironic to me that someone with no parenting experience was supposed to decide if we would be able to parent one more child.

At our first meeting, she said, "Tell me about your marriage."

I replied, "Well, it's up and down, like every marriage."

"What do you mean, up and down?" she asked.

I didn't know what to tell her, but I remember thinking, "Come back in a few years and you won't ask that." I went home and asked my friends, "Do you know what I mean by an up-and-down marriage?" They all knew exactly what I meant, but the social worker had no clue. She couldn't—she was too young. I guess we passed the interview anyway, because we got a referral soon afterward.

The agency sent us a picture of a tiny, two-and-a-half year old girl, sitting on the floor of the orphanage holding a sign that read "#9400." In the background were cribs and chamber pots, but no toys. They told us she had come to the orphanage six months previously, but that was all the information we received. Much later, we found out that she had been in another orphanage since she was forty-two days old and had been moved because she wasn't thriving. Her birth mother had taken her to the first orphanage when the man she planned to marry wouldn't marry her if she kept the baby, who was fathered by another man.

I wish the agency had told us all that they knew right up front. It would have been nice to know what to expect, rather than being thrown into it with nothing more than, "Oh, you're not going to have any problems." Her background didn't make any difference to us, but as our daughter got older and began to question her beginnings, especially during her teenage years, it would have been easier to have had all the facts right from the start.

We all went to New York City to pick her up at the airport—my husband and me, our three boys—who were eleven, seven, and five at the time—and my mother. We were part of a large group of adoptive families waiting to greet their children. I clasped her picture and looked for "#9400," scared and excited all at once. After all the regular passengers had disembarked, we heard a child crying, then our name announced, and then... there she was, looking small, tired, and miserable. I took her in my arms and the attendant placed my child's arms around my neck and whispered something in Korean. My brand new daughter stopped crying, looked at my face, then laid her head on my shoulder.

She came with no information or guidelines, so I really didn't know what to do. We had a four hour drive ahead of us, so we decided to start our new family adventure with chocolate ice cream at a nearby coffee shop. After we'd eaten, I took my daughter into the restroom, where she was fascinated by the running water. She kept smiling and patting me and pointing to it. My guess is they didn't have running water in the orphanage, or toilets either. She was already toilet-trained, but for a while, she would use any convenient receptacle.

The first few months were hard for all of us. She came home with two raging ear infections, so she was pretty miserable until her ears cleared up. Between the antibiotics and the new food, her system was so upset that she had diarrhea for three months. She understood only Korean; we spoke only English. We called her Linda, which, of course, she had never heard before. Even the furniture was strange to her. She squatted on her chair for a very long time. The surroundings and the people in her life were all completely different. She must have thought she'd gone to the moon, because it couldn't have been any more alien.

It's amazing, really, that she did as well as she did. She may have been afraid, but she was a real trouper. Whatever we did, she went along with it. If we went out to play in the snow, I'd think, "I'll just leave her in the play room with one of the boys." But she would put on her coat and follow us out into the snow. Those first few weeks were challenging and it must have been really hard on her, but she did her best and won us all over.

It is such a characteristic of Linda to simply deal with situations, to solve problems on her own. She may not come up with the best solution, but if something is not working, she tackles the problem. One time, the toilet was leaking, and we were all standing around wondering what to do. Linda went and got a little plastic bucket and put it under the leak to catch the water. None of us had thought of that. If she couldn't reach something, she would stack up whatever was handy to make a stool. She's always been independent. She trusts herself and doesn't look for help, which in some ways, has made her life harder. On her second day home, she slipped on the rug and fell down the stairs. We all rushed down behind her, but she just gave one cry, got up, dusted herself off, and went on. She never looked around for comfort or help. Maybe she would have been like that anyway, but I think she learned that self sufficiency very early in her life, in the orphanage. Those kinds of things never disappear entirely.

Maybe they didn't have enough food in the orphanage, because Linda acted like she was starving when she first came home. She never wasted a scrap of food. She could eat a bowl of soup without spilling a drop. Once, a little bit got on her chin, and she stuck out her tongue and carefully retrieved it. She did not waste even the smallest amount of food. If she dropped anything, she went down on the floor after it. And she was sneaky about taking any food that was left out and hoarding it. She was used to being hungry. She ate anything that fell on the floor, at home or in public. She ate the cat food. Things got better as she realized that the food source was stable. It actually helped the bonding process. When she realized I was the one that provided the food, I became her best friend.

Except for those first few weeks of adjustment, I've never thought of Linda as anyone other than my daughter. The rest of us are Caucasian, but I forget that Linda doesn't look like us. I just see her as my daughter, as herself. So when other people would make comments about it, it would startle me. Once, when she had only been home about a month, we were shopping and Linda scooted away and got into the elevator and the doors closed. It was scary, and a group of people were gathered around, saying, "There's a baby in there. Where's the mother?" Linda was too small to reach any buttons, so eventually the doors opened. I was trying to push my way through the crowd, saying, "Excuse me, I'm the mother." But Linda didn't know I was the mother, either, so she just stood there looking lost.

A year or so later, she and I were in a store and she kept wandering off, calling, "Mommy, mommy!" After the third time, I said to Linda, "Listen young lady, if you would stay with your mother, you wouldn't be lost." A woman marched over, took Linda by the hand, and said, "Don't worry, little girl, we'll find your mother." I just laughed and said, "I am her mother."

I don't know if it bothered her that she didn't look like us, but I think she recognized it right from the beginning. There was a little Asian girl in a science class that the boys were attending, and the first time Linda saw her, she went over and patted her and smiled. She was still only two years old. Later, we went to Cambridge, where there were a lot of Asians, and she kept patting people and saying, "Mommy, lookit, lookit!" She was obviously happy to see other Asians.

It surprised me how much prejudice Linda had to deal with in school. She got a lot of teasing, because she was the only Asian in her school. We would have family discussions at the dinner table about it, trying to help her figure out how to best handle it. One of the boys would say, "You should just punch 'em!" But someone else would counter, "No, because then you'll get a reputation for fighting." The conversation would go on in that vein, until it would usually boil down to, "Well, I think you'll just have to grin and bear it." I think the boys gained something valuable, in that they became aware of what it's like to deal with prejudice. They saw Linda as their sister, as a person, and that experience allowed them to see other people for themselves, no matter what they looked like.

The boys were thrilled to have a sister, and they bonded well with her. When Linda was a teenager, she would get annoyed when people didn't realize they were her brothers. If they were all out together somewhere, people would often assume she was one of their dates.

Linda would come home and tell me indignantly, "Like I would go out with this guy?"

Linda had some rough years as a teenager. She was very bitter toward her birth parents for giving her up. She took it personally, because of course, to her, it was personal. I kept telling her, "It wasn't you. They didn't even know you. There's nothing wrong with you." I tried to help her focus on the family who really wanted her, but I'm not sure I succeeded in that.

There's no way to honestly make any general remarks about the difference between raising biological children and adopted children. So much depends on the child. Many biological children struggle as teenagers and the same is true of adopted children. Adoptees have the additional burden of dealing with some deeper questions of identity, and sometimes that can be very painful. As a parent, all you can do is muddle through the best you can, loving your child the best way you know how.

I cannot imagine our family without Linda. She brought a great balance to the family, and I have always been happy that she is ours. The boys learned a lot of things from her, because she knows how to stand up for what she wants. She's a wonderful person—very smart, witty, and creative. She's a mother herself now—to three smart, witty, creative children.

Parenting is *the* great adventure. You never know how the family dynamics will work. You never know whether to attribute something to heredity or environment. You wonder what's due to nature, and what to nurture, especially in adoption. But I never could see the point of worrying about it. I just dealt with whatever came up the best way I knew how, simply because Linda is my daughter and I love her.

Bill

"My relationship with Dad is totally different from the relationship I had with my biological father. I carried both of my fathers around in my heart for a long time."

Prior to my father's death, my family consisted of myself, my father, my younger brother, and my mom. We were the typical suburban family unit. Then my dad got cancer and died just after my ninth birthday.

I was mystified by his death. I knew something was wrong with him, because he was in the hospital and we would go visit him there. I watched the metamorphosis in him, as the cancer and the chemotherapy affected his body. He gained weight and all his hair fell out. He just wasn't the same person that played with us and pushed us on the swing, helped us build a tree fort and taught me how to ride a bike. I would look at him lying in that hospital bed and it was like he wasn't my daddy anymore. He was just a person in a hospital bed that looked very familiar to me, and yet so different that I felt some sort of separation. Maybe I detached myself from it because I looked so much like him, even as a kid. It didn't change what I felt about him, but my perception of him was much different than it had been.

We talked about his illness within the family, but there wasn't a sense of impending doom. Then one day, my brother and I were walking home from school and we noticed that our driveway was full of cars. "Something's up," my brother said.

"Yeah, I wonder what's going on," I said, as we came through our front door.

The house was full of people. My mother took us into my bedroom and we all sat on the bed. To this day, I remember all the details of that moment—what the carpet looked like, the smells in the air. She told us that our daddy was dead. The three of us huddled together and cried and cried.

I do have some vivid memories of my father, but they're like short flashes of light, snapshots of my early life. I remember the smell of his aftershave and the way his car sounded when he pulled into the garage. I remember him fondly, although my mother tells me that he was a little rough on me—not in an abusive way, but in the way he tried to make me a man. But I don't remember any of that, which is strange.

I could tell that my father's death affected my mother more than it did me. Nothing in my life changed radically. We lived in the same house. I still went to school and played with my buddies and watched TV on Friday night. I spent a lot of time at my grandparents' house—my mom's folks. Life wasn't the same without my dad, but the day-to-day living didn't change much.

Some months later, my mom started dating. I knew she was dating, but I didn't think much about it. I was only nine years old, after all. Then she started going out with a man named Bill, and he became something of a regular in our lives. Things seemed to be getting better and better until one day, mom announced that "we" were getting married again. She meant the three of us, as a family unit.

This all happened pretty fast, while I was still in a bit of a funk over my father's death. Looking back on it, I think Mom knew well before my father died that he was not going to live. It makes me wonder if she had already begun to detach herself from him a little bit, not because she didn't love him with all her heart, but because she knew that at the end of the day, she would be alone. And Bill was not a stranger to her. He and his father had built our house, so she already knew him.

I liked Bill. So the proposal of marriage sounded all right to me. Though he was radically different from my father, he was always respectful and courteous to my mom. That meant a lot to me, even at my tender age. As the oldest son, I was the man of the family now, and I was fiercely loyal and protective of my mother. At the wedding, my brother and I gave her away. He was seven years old and I had just turned ten.

All of a sudden, I was part of a new family and it felt a little foreign to me. Bill's folks and his family really embraced me and my brother. We were the only grandchildren in the family, and we had come half-grown, so maybe they were making up for lost time. We felt very welcome, but it was still strange to think of all these new people as family.

A couple of months after the wedding, Bill adopted me and my brother. It was a beautiful spring day and we all went down to the county courthouse. Sunlight was streaming through the windows of the judge's chambers. My brother and I sat next to the judge and he asked us, "Okay, boys, do you really want to do this?" We didn't know any better, so we said, "Of course we do." I could tell this was a big deal. It's not every day that you get to have a chat with a judge.

Of course, my mom had talked to us about it. She explained adoption this way: "Bill won't be your biological father, but on paper, he will be your legal father, so there won't be any of this stepparent business. Your relationship with him won't change, but the legalities will. He will treat you the same way he always has. We are not throwing away the memory of your father, but it would mean a lot to Bill if you would become his legal sons. It would mean a lot to me, too."

I was ten years old, trying to figure it all out, but what I did understand made sense to me. I had friends who had stepparents and that was hard for them. So adoption seemed preferable to me. My brother was only seven and not very clear about the whole thing. "What are you going to do, Bill?" he asked. I said, "I think we should be adopted. It will make us more of a real family unit."

That was a good day, the day we were adopted. A real good day. It was just as good as the day my dad died had been bad. A lot of our extended family was with us to celebrate. We all went out to dinner after we'd finished at the courthouse, then everyone came over to our house. Yes, that was a happy day.

My name changed that same day. I walked into the courthouse as William Stewart Stradley and when I walked out, my name was William Benton Kinney, III, after Bill. That was a big deal, and it felt kind of funky, for lack of a better word. I had a new social security number and everything. I felt like I was a whole different person. Yet when my friends freaked out about it, I said, "I'm still Bill, for crying out loud! I'm not a different person." But I did feel different.

I'm not sure why I agreed to change my name, but I think I subconsciously reasoned, "I'm not disrespecting my father, because he's gone. Mom has taken Bill's name, and because it's important to her that I do this, it's important to me." Over the years, it has meant more and more to me. As my relationship with Bill developed and he became my Dad, my new name became more and more important to me. It means a lot to me that he was willing to share his name with me.

After the adoption, my brother and I still called our new father "Bill," like we always had. Then one day, I started calling him "Dad." Nobody forced the issue. He was a father figure to me. Even if he had not adopted me and even if I had not taken his name, he was still a very strong male figure in my life. He used to joke, "I'm glad I came along when I did, or you guys would have turned into Mama's boys, and that would have been pretty messy."

My relationship with Dad is totally different from the relationship I had with my biological father, whom I had called "Daddy." I carried both of my fathers around in my heart for a long time. To some extent, I still do, though my feelings for my birth father have faded over the years. My feelings for him are completely different from my feelings for Dad, because I only knew him as a child. When I think of my biological father, I'm sad sometimes, because he's not ever coming back. But I don't spend time reliving that part of my life. I was a child, and now that's over.

I look so much like my birth father that I occasionally have trouble knowing who I am. I can't escape the mirror. My resemblance to my biological father sometimes frightens people who knew him. When I was about twenty, working my way through college as a waiter, my appearance shocked a lot of customers who had known my father. One guy stared at me during his whole meal and finally asked, "Is your name Bill Stradley?" I told him, "Yeah, it used to be. He was my father." He said, "You scared the hell out of me. I thought I was seeing a ghost."

However, I don't identify myself as the son of Bill Stradley. If you ask me who my dad is, I'll point to Bill Kinney, Jr. I won't even think to tell you, "My dad has been dead for twenty years." It's not an issue, except for people who knew Bill Stradley. I'm a Kinney. I may not be genetically connected to Bill Kinney, but I am his son.

It was a little tough coming into adolescence with a new father. I was just a normal little boy, then I experienced death and remarriage and adoption and a name change, and soon thereafter began undergoing fairly radical changes physically, mentally, and psychologically. I had more trouble than most with the whole identity issue. I felt lost for a long time. But I think the name change made a big difference in helping me connect with my new identity as Bill Kinney. I look like my birth father, but I share a name with my adoptive father, and he's the one that is here for me now.

The greatest benefit to being adopted has been having a strong male figure in my life. I have friends who really struggle because of the lack of a father figure. I feel very fortunate that I have Dad. I have the utmost respect for single parents, but I think children really need that yin/yang in their lives. I admire Dad for doing what he did. That's a huge thing, to marry a woman with two kids, to step up to the plate and say, "Okay, this is a package deal and I'm willing to take it on." He accepted me as his son, gave me his name, and raised me as his own. In some respects, I'm a lot like him, and in other ways, I'm not. I think that's a byproduct of having both of my fathers influence my life. But I'm very grateful for Dad. What I've learned from him, I wouldn't trade for anything.

Lisa

"I feel extremely honored to be part of the world of adoption. It alters lives forever. It creates 'forever families.' What a privilege to be part of that!"

I have seven children—three by birth and four by adoption. When my youngest biological child was six, my husband and I decided we wanted to even out our family with two girls and two boys. So we decided to adopt a little girl.

Adoption has been part of my dreams and desires for as long as I can remember. By the time I was twelve years old, I knew I wanted to adopt a child internationally. The only international adoptions happening then were from Korea, so at my eighth grade graduation, I announced my plans for the future, "I am going to adopt two little girls from Korea."

I'm not sure why international adoption was planted in my heart at such an early age, but I do know that each of my children are meant to be in my family. So when the time was right, international adoption was a natural step for me. I was unclear about which country my child would come from, but I did know we would adopt internationally.

My husband and I chose India for our first adoption, because that is where the need for adoptive families was greatest. We applied through a local adoption agency and about a year later, received an assignment. Our new daughter, Sarah, came home in the summertime, at eight weeks old. Many of the babies coming out of India at that time weighed only three or four pounds, and the orphanages tried to get them to their families as quickly as possible because of their fragile health. At a healthy seven pounds, Sarah was a fortunate exception. She was a dream come true and we enjoyed her so much we decided to adopt again.

A year or so later, some friends of ours were trying to adopt a little boy from Guatemala, but the adoption fell through in the midst of a scandal that took place in Guatemala during the processing of their case. Though they went on to adopt a different child, that little boy remained in my heart. I called the agency and said, "If you can find this little boy, we would really like to adopt him." As they searched for him, Janet, the Latin America Program Director, offered to show me pictures of other waiting children. I told her I did not want to see the pictures, because I knew if I saw the faces of those precious children, I would want to bring home more than one child. And I did.

The agency never could locate the little boy, but when I finally looked at the photos of waiting children, I saw a picture of a little two-year-old girl with beautiful curls and a rosebud mouth that just captured my heart. Then I saw a picture of a tiny two-year-old boy with a sweet smile, and I wanted him, too. There was something wrong with his back, so he wasn't as physically developed as most children his age, but we were told it was a correctable handicap.

My husband and I began the legal process to adopt both children. We made arrangements with Shriners Hospital, so that when we brought them home, we would be ready to attend to their medical needs. We knew our daughter, Mary, would require special care because she had had polio as a baby and it had affected one of her legs. But we didn't know exactly what Jess, our new son, would need.

Janet went with me to Guatemala to pick up my children. When I met Jess and Mary for the first time, I was overwhelmed and flooded with emotion. I could immediately see that Jess had an uncorrectable disability, later diagnosed as cerebral palsy. As the reality of what we'd signed up for began to sink in, I realized I may have taken on more than I could handle. I had a two-year-old at home already, and I could see that Jess and Mary would require a lot more time and energy than I had anticipated. Life was not going to be easy.

Jess and Mary came home very traumatized from living in a state-run orphanage where they had not been treated well. In addition, they had just lost everything that was important and familiar to them. Hurting, frightened, and feeling alone, neither of them were ready to trust me, the complete stranger who had taken them away from the only home they knew. Mary frequently stood in the corner, shaking, and could not find comfort in my touch. When a stranger entered the room, Jess would sometimes tremble, as though he were afraid of being hit.

Those first few years were very difficult. The children struggled in a totally new environment, where the people, the food, the language, and even the smells were all strange to them. Because they had been given so little power up to that point in their young lives, control became a huge issue. Jess would usually disregard our requests and do the opposite of what we asked. This was a very challenging time for our family, but we also experienced tremendous growth in faith, courage, and strength.

I did everything I could think of to be the parent these children needed, from reading piles of books to attending numerous conferences. I had always thought of myself as a loving mom who could love any child, and the child would soon love me back. But it didn't work that way with these two. At night, for instance, they would not cry for someone to come when they were scared or needed something. Sometimes I would check on them in their beds and find them wide awake, staring at the ceiling. They had obviously learned early that no one would come, even if they did cry. As their mother, I longed to soothe their pain and comfort their fears, but they couldn't trust me enough to let me. It broke my heart, because I felt I couldn't give them what they needed.

As a result of my extensive reading, many conferences, and conversations with other adoptive mothers, I learned a lot about attachment issues and how to parent children who do not trust. I soon realized that I was the one who needed to change. I had to adjust my attitudes, my expectations, and my actions. When I did, the children modified their behavior in response. In some ways, I was more permissive with Jess and Mary than I was with my other children. But they needed that generous acceptance, that feeling of being loved for who they are, free of demands to fit into someone else's idea of a successful person. Such unconditional love is important for every child, but for Jess and Mary, it was critical. Of course, the trick is to keep that in balance with teaching them how to behave in the family and in society.

Although those first few years with Jess and Mary were a real struggle, their adolescent years were comparatively easy. They were in special education all through their school years, and even though they are still considered "special needs," they both have good jobs and meaningful relationships. They have grown into sweet, considerate adults, and though they will probably always deal with issues of trust, both Jess and Mary are happy, well-adjusted, contributing members of their family and their community.

About two years after Jess and Mary came home, Janet called from the adoption agency and said, "I have a little boy that I think is yours."

"What?! I don't think so!" I exclaimed.

"He's about two years old and he has some emotional problems," she continued. "Since you have experience with children dealing with loss and abandonment issues, I thought he'd do well in your family. He really needs a home."

"Well, you'd better find him a home elsewhere, because six is enough for us. We're feeling quite complete as a family."

"Even so," Janet countered, "I'm going to keep him on hold for a while, because I really think he's yours."

I was a stay-at-home mom at that point, spending most of my time in the bathroom with three toddlers and handfuls of M&M's, trying to convince them what a great invention the toilet was. I had no aspirations to add a seventh child.

Two weeks after Janet called, I traveled to Guatemala with a friend to pick up the two children she was adopting. When we arrived at the orphanage, they brought out a little blond boy with big brown eyes that looked a lot like my biological sons and was about the same age as my three adopted children. It was the little boy Janet thought should be ours. I knew as soon as I saw him that she was right. I felt certain he was mine. He seemed to be a healthy child, but I could see that he was a very unhappy little boy.

I went home and told my husband about him, and he agreed that we needed to adopt him. I called Janet and admitted, "You're right. He's ours." Nine months later, I went back to Guatemala to bring our new son home.

When I went to the orphanage to pick up Matthew, he took one look at me and ran out of the room, yelling, "No Mama!" We had to resort to bribery to convince him to go with me, and with the promise of a Pepsi, we were on our way. As soon as we got home, an amazing transformation took place. Matthew started skipping down the hallway, happy as could be, and parenting him has been a wonderfully easy, painless experience. Of course, my perception may be somewhat skewed by the taxing years I spent with my first children from Guatemala. Many things seem effortless in comparison!

In international adoption, birth parents are a hugely important, but mysterious piece of the adoption triad. All of my adopted children have talked about their birth parents at certain stages of their lives. None of them have any way of ever finding their biological families, and that is a great loss for each of them. Information about their birth parents is a gift I would love to have given them.

When she was young, Sarah seemed to feel a deep connection to her birth mother. She would walk hand-in-hand with me and tell me, "I want you to know I love you just as much as my birth mother." She talked about her birth mother quite freely until she came to believe that she would come to live with us someday. When I told her, "Honey, we don't even know who your birth mother is," her dream of a reunion died, and she didn't mention her birth mother for a long time. For many years, she was afraid to return to India, but now looks forward to visiting the country of her birth.

Mary's birth mother left her at a babysitter's house and never returned to pick her up, and Mary speaks freely of the circumstances surrounding her adoption. Jess, on the other hand, had to work through a lot of anger about his history. When he was young, he would tell people that his parents threw him into a garbage can, but I kept reassuring him that that was not true. He was left at a hospital, and my guess is that his parents knew he had medical needs they were simply too poor to handle.

Matthew didn't talk about his adoption much when he was younger, but now he's very open about his adoption story and is comfortable with having it be a part of who he is. He was found on the street and taken to the orphanage, so we are not even sure of his age. Because he hated the orphanage and adjusted so easily to family life, I think he must have had a parent who loved him early in his life.

Self-esteem is an essential part of every child's development, but I think it must be nurtured more diligently in children who have been adopted. We made a conscious effort to promote a strong sense of self through working together as a family and participating in Culture Camps and other gatherings of adoptive families. This gave our children a chance to see other normal, happy families who had also come together by adoption, and they developed some close relationships with other adopted kids that shared similar experiences. In addition, we brought items from their native countries into our home and made those a significant part of our lives.

When my children were all still very young, a major event brought drastic change to our lives. After almost twenty years of marriage, my husband and I divorced, which devastated our entire family. We were keenly aware that our adopted sons and daughters had already lost their birth parents, so we tried to maintain as much stability as we could for all the children by having them live with me and arranging frequent visits with their father.

Several years later, I began dating a terrific man that I really cared for. As the relationship deepened and we began discussing marriage, I explained that I was a "package deal," that my children came first in my life. I knew I needed a dedicated partner who would accept my kids and participate in their lives. We needed someone we could count on; he needed time to think things over.

He called me one day to ask for a ride to the hospital, after an accident at work. When my children heard about his accident, they were very concerned and insisted on becoming his caretakers, since he did not have anyone else nearby to assist him in his recovery. They took meals to him and made sure his needs were met. They melted his heart with their generosity. He finally said to me, with tears in his eyes, "I love you. And I love your kids. Let's get married."

Six months later, my children and I welcomed Mark into our family as husband and step-dad. It was similar to another adoption. And like every adoption, the adjustment has not always been easy, but the blessings abound. Mark is deeply committed to our family and we know we can rely on him.

My training in social work and my personal experiences with adoption eventually led to my career in the field. I believe adoption is a wonderful way to bring children into a family, but there are issues that often surface, especially when adopting older or special-needs children. I wanted to help educate and prepare prospective parents, so I volunteered to teach the pre-adoption classes at the agency that had helped with my four adoptions. I discovered that I had a passion for supporting adoptive parents both before and after their child comes home, so I began to look into career opportunities.

When my children were all in school, I got a job at a domestic adoption agency and worked there for three years. I facilitated reunions between adoptees and birth parents and also brought babies from the hospital to their new parents.

Then I went back to school and began working in the field of disabilities, supporting parents whose children had recently been diagnosed with a disability. One day, I received a call from a local international adoption agency asking if I would accept a position there as Director of Social Services. Satisfied with the work I was doing, I said, "No, thanks." But they were persistent and persuasive, and when I finally went in for an interview, I enthusiastically said, "Yes."

In my new role, I coordinated home studies and post-placement reports and provided follow-up support to families. When the agency Director left, I was asked to step into her position. I struggled with the decision because I knew it would mean long hours, incredible responsibility, and big changes to every part of my life. But my passion for adoption work outweighed any negative aspects, so I have been serving as the agency Director for several years now.

My job is a roller coaster of heartache and joy. I have traveled all over the world and seen many homeless, suffering children. But I also get to see children coming home to families, home to the love and security that they deserve. Our agency's humanitarian work in several countries is a source of satisfaction, as well, as we impact whole villages in positive ways. As I expected, the work is busy, demanding, and sometimes frustrating, but incredibly rewarding.

I have learned so much about human nature, unconditional love, and the power of prayer through all my experience with adoption. I can't imagine my life without my adopted children; they have enriched my life beyond measure. My biological children have benefitted, as well, and it is gratifying to see the circle continue, as my oldest daughter has adopted two little girls from India. I feel extremely honored to be part of the world of adoption. It alters lives forever. It creates "forever families." What a privilege to be a part of that!

Crystle

*"Like every birth mother, I loved my babies and didn't want
to let them go. But that's exactly why I was determined to
place my twins with Tim and Judy. I truly loved my babies
and wanted what was best for them."*

I was fourteen when I found out I was pregnant. My boyfriend was
twenty-seven and in and out of jail, so he wasn't very involved with
the whole thing. I told him I was pregnant, but I didn't tell my
mother for quite a while. I was living with a friend and his parents at
the time, so I was very rarely home. I was a pretty rebellious child.

As soon as the at-home pregnancy test confirmed my suspicions, I
thought, "Okay, now I need to go to the doctor." Strangely, I wasn't
scared or worried. It just didn't feel that important, at the time. I was
in a fog, and I really didn't think much about it. Nothing was real. I
lived in a dream world and I could only concentrate on getting through
one day at a time.

At the doctor's office, the doctor did a sonogram. She listened,
perplexed, and asked, "Do twins run in your family?"

"No," I replied.

She told me, "I'm going to schedule an ultrasound for you."

"Okay. Why?"

"I hear two heartbeats," she announced.

I was speechless. And suddenly scared. I looked up at her and finally squeaked, "No! That's not okay!" A couple of weeks later, the ultrasound confirmed that I was carrying twins.

I was being tutored by a teacher from the public school and I thank God I had her. She got me through everything. I told her right away what was going on. She said, "Let's go to the library and start researching options." We got some books on adoption and learned about all the different ways you can do an adoption. I never considered having an abortion. I can't say that I wouldn't now, but at that time, it didn't even cross my mind.

I thought about keeping the babies—for a split second. If it had been one baby, I might have thought more about it. But I wasn't even old enough to go out and get a job. There was no way I could take care of two babies. And I did want to finish school. So it was never a huge, agonizing decision for me. Adoption was the obvious choice.

I was still in a dream-like state, just swimming through the experience a day at a time. Nancy, my tutor, helped me find all the adoption options, lay them out on the table, then let me make up my own mind about how I wanted to proceed. After we had done some research, I decided I wanted to do an open adoption. So Nancy made a list of local agencies that did open adoptions and told me to call them to set up appointments, so I could get a better idea of what an open adoption would really entail.

I didn't know much about open adoption, going into this. I knew how a partially-open adoption worked, where the birth mother gets letters and pictures, but no visits. For me, closed adoption was definitely out. I didn't want my babies growing up wondering about their heritage. I grew up without knowing my own father and I would have liked to know something about him, even just background information. I'm sure that experience influenced my decision.

I began calling the agencies on the list and most of the people I talked to were almost rude. One lady told me, "Well, you need to call so-and-so and set up an appointment with them." I was just a fourteen-year-old kid trying to get some help and still feeling like this wasn't really happening to me. So any little obstacle seemed huge to me.

I finally connected with an agency with really nice people. We set up a time to meet, and Nancy and I went and talked to a counselor about what an open adoption would be like and the steps involved in making it happen. The counselor gave me some packets to take home and look at—letters and pictures of families wanting to adopt. She told me to pick out a few that I liked and then come back to get more information on those people.

I looked at all the pictures and read a lot of letters. One photo really stood out from the rest. It was the only picture that wasn't posed. It was a snapshot of a smiling couple, and they looked so happy. I went back to the agency and got three or four big, thick packets—including the "happy couple" packet. Theirs was the only packet I read all the way through. I just knew they were my family.

They were looking for twins. Actually, I noticed that most of the prospective parents wanted twins. "Twins preferred" was a common phrase in the letters I read. I guess if people know they want more than one child, it's easier to do one adoption and get both children at once.

I met Tim and Judy shortly before I went into labor. They lived two hours away, but they drove up to meet me at the agency. I was nervous, but when they admitted that they were anxious, too, I relaxed. From that very first meeting, I absolutely loved them. They are very happy, wonderful people.

About this time, the reality of what I was doing hit me. I had been in a dream world for quite a while, not really taking any of it seriously. Then I went through the "cool stage," where my dominant thoughts ran something like, "Hey, everybody, look at me! I'm pregnant—with twins! Aren't I cool?" I thought everybody should pay attention to me and take care of me.

But a couple of weeks before the birth, it suddenly hit me, "Oh my gosh, what the heck am I doing? I'm pregnant—with twins!" My little dream world suddenly went *whoosh*, like air out of a balloon. I started to think about things more seriously at that point. I'd seen teenagers keep children that they couldn't take care of. Every time I'd see a situation like that, I'd feel so terrible for the kids. I knew that my kids would have a horrible time if I even attempted to raise them. I was too young. And there were two of them! Like every birth mother, I loved my babies and didn't want to let them go. But that's exactly why I was determined to place my twins with Tim and Judy. I truly loved my babies, and I wanted what was best for them. All along, I knew that the wisest, most loving choice was adoption.

I was thirty-one weeks pregnant when I went into labor. My doctor put me in the hospital and the medical staff did what they could to keep the babies in as long as possible. It worked for a week. But then the doctors determined that one of the babies wasn't getting sufficient nourishment, and I developed a uterine infection, so they tried to get them out as soon as possible. From my perspective, it was a sudden, strange reversal and I was scared. I thought I'd have more time to prepare for birth. I had done some reading about childbirth, but I hadn't been to any classes. I really didn't know what to expect.

There were several complications at birth, both for me and the babies. I was in an operating room, so the doctors could be ready for an emergency Caesarean birth. One twin was breech. My mom was with me, and my doctor, plus a whole room full of people I didn't know. Tim and Judy were out in the hall. Looking back on it, I don't know why I didn't have them come in for the birth. Tim is a surgeon and it was kind of silly of me to make them wait outside. But I wasn't thinking of that, at the time.

Luckily, the epidural worked great. And the boys were quite small—only three pounds each—so the actual birth wasn't too difficult. I was really out of it afterwards, though, and I think I scared a lot of people that night, since I had some major problems during those first few hours after birth.

I didn't even see my baby boys for the first couple of days. I couldn't leave my room and they were in incubators in the neonatal intensive care unit, so they couldn't go visiting either. I did get to spend some time with them before I left the hospital. And I came back to see them a few times after I'd been released, because they had to stay in the hospital for about two months.

It was very difficult for me to see them, both physically and emotionally. I would hold them, but they were so small, and they had wires sticking out of various parts, so even that was hard. It was difficult to believe that these were my children, that they had come out of me, that we were related by blood.

I would sit and hold them and think, "This is it. They're going to go home with Tim and Judy and they'll take wonderful care of them and my boys are going to be happy." I never had any regrets about what I had decided to do. Never. I knew I was doing the wisest thing I could do. I felt a huge relief—and a deep gratitude—that they were going to be well taken care of. I was so glad my boys wouldn't have to deal with me trying to care for them, because I knew I was in no position to do it. Even though it has always been hard for me to see them, I have never regretted placing them with Tim and Judy. I didn't really have much of a problem giving them up. I knew that adoption was the best way to show my sons how much I loved them.

The boys are six years old now. It is still very difficult and very emotional for me to go see them. The first time I went to visit, I took the train to their house, planning to stay a couple of nights. But as I sat on the couch bottle-feeding the babies, I started crying and couldn't stop. I don't know why. Tim and Judy comforted me and helped me arrange to go home early.

Over the years, the visits have become easier. We have a lot of fun. I see them two or three times a year, but if they lived closer, and if my schedule were not so crazy, I would love to see them more often. It is so gratifying to see my boys growing up in such a wonderful family. Tim and Judy have since adopted two more children and are considering another adoption. My relationship with them is very warm, very open. I love their whole family, and I know they love me, too.

Choosing adoption helped me get on with my life. I grew up. It was almost like a near-death experience. Before I got pregnant, my life was a real mess and I wasn't headed anywhere good. I feel like I got a second chance, and I'm doing everything I can to make something good of my life. I'm an incredibly different person. I dropped out of school at fourteen, and now I'm in college. I had never even planned to go to college, but after the boys were born, I was determined to go.

I came out of this experience very clear about what I don't want in life. I'm still not sure exactly what I do want—I'm two years into college and still haven't chosen a major. But at least I know what I don't want my life to look like. I know I'm doing good things for myself, and I'm happy about the way my life is going.

I've seen so many people ruin not only their lives, but their children's lives, as well, by keeping kids they can't care for. Of course it hurts to let them go. But if you think about your children instead of your own pain, it becomes so much easier. You realize what a gift you are giving your children, to find them a wonderful family that can give them the life they deserve. And you can still be a part of your child's life. A big part. A lot of adoptive parents really want the birth parents to be around. Open adoption is a win/win/win situation.

To tell the truth, I'm actually rather impressed with myself. Adoption was one of the smartest decisions I've ever made. Sometimes when people find out about my boys, they'll tiptoe around me, like they're afraid I'll burst into tears if we talk about it. But I have no regrets. I'm very proud of my boys. And I'm proud of myself for having enough love and intelligence to do the right thing for them.

© Holt International Children's Services

Rachel

"My story is sad, in a lot of respects, but the challenges I faced were not related to being adopted. There are no perfect families."

I don't know much about the circumstances of my birth except that I was born somewhere in South Korea. I do remember my brother's birth. I was two-and-a-half years old and I remember coming home from the hospital with him. But my mother did not come home, because she had died.

My brother and I lived with our father, who was an alcoholic. When I was quite young, he would send me to the store to buy alcohol for him. It was a terrible situation. Then my father became ill and sent me to the country to live with some aunts. There was a younger aunt, who was about sixty years old, and a really old aunt. My brother must have been sent somewhere else, but I don't know where he was.

I enjoyed living in the country. My aunts were kind to me, and it was a relief not to have to deal with my father's alcoholism. I remember going to town one summer day with my younger aunt, and she bought me a popsicle. On the way home, my nose started to bleed, so she slapped the popsicle on the back of my neck to stop the bleeding.

I must have been there in the fall, too, because the persimmons were ripe. My aunts and I gathered all the ripe persimmons and put them in jars. Then we dug holes in the ground and put the jars of persimmons in the ground, to store them over winter.

When I was sent back to the city, I was sad. I was losing everyone—my mother, my brother, and now these two kind aunts. Then, when I arrived back in the city, I was informed that my father had died, so my brother and I were now orphans.

My aunts were simply too old to care for us, and there was no one else in our extended family willing or able to take us. So it was decided that my brother and I would be given up for adoption.

One of our uncles, a man we didn't really know, drove us in his cab to the train station to catch the train to the orphanage. My brother didn't understand what was happening. He threw up in the cab, which made my uncle angry. I knew where we were going, but I didn't know exactly what it would entail. I did understand that we were being sent away again, that our parents were both dead, and that there was nobody to take care of us. I was six years old.

There were a lot of children in the orphanage, the oldest of which was a thirteen-year-old girl. She had actually gone to live with a family and then been sent back. That's all I knew about that, but we all noticed who came and went. There was a big room for the girls and a big room for the boys, and we had a nanny that stayed with us, even at night. We sat at long tables for meals and ate lots of soup. There was no schooling and I don't remember seeing any books there. We didn't take baths very often, but when we did, we all used one big tub. The girls bathed first, so the water wasn't very dirty or cold by the time I had my turn, but my poor little brother had to wait until all the girls were done before he stood in the cold water for his bath.

I watched and worried over my brother. He would call for our mother most nights in the orphanage and once, he ran away. I was scared, because I didn't think they would find him. He was only four years old. But they brought him back and I guess he resigned himself to the fact that nobody was coming to get us.

We lived at the orphanage for about two years. I remember snowball fights in the winters and one summer, some soldiers came to visit. Maybe they were American, because we were taught some songs in English to perform for them. Later, when my mom taught me *London Bridge is Falling Down*, I recognized it as one of the songs we had sung for the soldiers.

One day the nanny showed me a letter and said, "It looks like there's a family that wants to adopt you and your brother." I didn't feel particularly excited or scared at the news, though I did wonder what it would be like. And I was glad for something new.

My mom tells a whole story about how she found us: *Your father and I had been looking for our children for a long time. Twelve years before we found you and your brother, I was fasting and praying because I wanted to have children. I had a personal revelation that I was going to adopt three children. I even knew what your names were to be. So I looked for my three children for a long time. I finally realized that you might not all come together, so first we adopted you and your brother, and then we found your youngest brother in India.*

It was March when my brother and I left Korea and came to Hawaii to live with our adoptive parents. We were bundled up in snowsuits because it was very cold in Korea. Then the plane landed in Hawaii and the lady escorting us took us into the bathroom and had us change into some nice clothes before we met our parents.

I was nervous. I didn't know what to think about what was happening. I understood that we were going to live with these people, but I don't think I really understood the implications.

After we met my parents, we went out to lunch, which was a horrible experience. Sandwiches were completely foreign to me, and I couldn't figure out how to eat mine. Besides, it tasted very strange. So I went hungry that day, even after lunch.

My parents lived in a big, two-story house. When I walked in the door and headed up the carpeted stairs, I thought, "We must be in a big hotel or something." It was so far out of my experience. Then I saw a big chandelier right at the top of the stairs and decided, "Oh, maybe it's a palace." I was in an awestruck, wondering-what-will-happen-next state of mind when my parents' dog came bounding up the stairs and began chasing us. That quickly broke the mood. My little brother ran 'round and 'round and knocked over a huge urn, breaking it, and my parents laughed and laughed.

The transition to American life and to a new family was a bit awkward. I hoarded food for a long time. We must have been short on food at the orphanage, so I was accustomed to worrying that there wouldn't be enough. I used to tuck little bits of food in my underwear drawer or some other secret place, just in case. My mom kept telling me that I didn't need to take food away from the table, but it took me a long time before I trusted that food would always be available.

My brother learned English faster than I did. But over the summer, I gradually replaced all my Korean words with English ones, so that by the time school started in the fall, I spoke fairly good English, although I didn't understand everything. I started school in second grade, in remedial classes, so I could work on my English. My mother worked with us, too, since she is an educator.

In those early days, I was very protective of my brother. I watched over him all the time. I made sure he ate. It drove my parents crazy when I would speak to him in Korean because to them, it sounded like I was lecturing him.

There was a point when I began to think of my new parents as Mom and Dad. I don't remember how long that took, but after a while, they were simply our parents. I had a few memories of my birth mother and I had very strong memories of my father, so it wasn't like I forgot about them. I think my brother bonded with our new parents better than I did. I felt about them like I imagine anyone feels about their parents—that I could trust them to take care of me. I don't have anything to compare it to, so it's hard to say. I felt the same way about them as I had felt toward my natural father, and I wasn't very close to him either. He always had to be taken care of.

My story gets very sad at this point, because my adoptive family was not the perfect family you might imagine. It was actually a very dysfunctional family, but I didn't realize that until I went to college and began to get a broader picture of life. It was just the way my life was, complete with sexual abuse and my parents' problems with addiction and depression.

When I was seventeen, my mother tried to commit suicide, and that's when I first talked to someone about the sexual abuse that was going on. Apparently, my mother thought that I should have kept the family secrets, and she and I haven't had a real relationship since then. My father has apologized to me, and I've accepted that. We keep trying to reconcile, but it gets to a certain point and just blows up. So my only contact with them, at this point, is through my youngest brother, who gets along with them fairly well. My parents haven't even met my daughter, which makes me very sad.

For all I've lost, however, I've gained some things. If I hadn't been adopted, I would never have received the religious training that I did, and even though there was a big discrepancy between what I was being taught and what was actually happening in our home, I have benefitted greatly from those teachings. And there's no way I would have had the educational opportunities I've had here in America had I stayed in Korea. My parents took us on family trips and exposed us to many different things. We had great opportunities to explore whatever we wanted, and they heartily supported all our interests. From an educational standpoint, my mother taught us well, which allowed me to graduate from college at eighteen and from medical school at twenty-two. So I did come to a point where I decided that even though I would not have chosen to go through all that I did, good things still came of it.

What really changed my perspective was my marriage and the birth of my daughter. My husband's family is very stable and loving, and that has been good for me to experience. And I had no idea that you could love a person as much as I love my little daughter. All kinds of healing and growth are happening now.

I do have some identity issues, but I don't think it's because I'm adopted. It has more to do with being Korean in a mostly-white society. I think of myself as white. I know I'm Korean, but I never think of myself as different until I notice an odd little reaction from someone and then I remember, "Oh, yeah, I don't really look like they do."

I think about this issue more since my daughter has been born, because I don't want her to be totally clueless about her cultural background. Growing up, my brothers and I were exposed to the

Hawaiian culture, but that's totally different from Korean or Indian culture, which we were not exposed to at all. We integrated very well into American society, but I lost that connection to my own heritage.

Although I do think about my birth family, I haven't had a burning desire to delve into my Korean genealogy. I am more curious than I used to be, though. One of these days, I may go to Korea and try to open my records—visit the orphanage where I lived, find out my original name, look for some hospital records. My brother spent some time in Korea, but he didn't do any family research. He did come back changed by the exposure to Korean culture, however, and I think he's better for it.

My story is sad, in a lot of respects, but the challenges I faced were not related to being adopted. There are no perfect families. I'm reminded of that all the time in my work as an Emergency Room physician. I'm very suspicious of people and always wonder what's really going on when I see a supposedly well-adjusted, happy family. If I hadn't seen my husband's family deal with one another with love and respect, even at their worst, I could not have believed it possible to have a happy family. That's not been my life's experience, until recently. But I have faith in the future. I have such hope in my daughter. Life is good now. I'm finally happy.

Kevin

*"When people ask me how long it took for us to adopt a
baby, I say, 'Oh, about eight hours.'"*

I am the rector of an Episcopal Church in the San Francisco Bay
Area. One day, Rick, a parishioner of mine, informed me that his
sixteen-year-old son, Justin, had gotten his girlfriend pregnant.
Justin lived out of state with his mother, but he would come visit his
father in the summertime, so I had known him for about seven years.

Justin and his girlfriend, Kristina, decided to keep the baby and
raise it together. When their families kicked them out of their homes
over the pregnancy, both kids were suddenly homeless and scared, so
Rick and his wife, Julie, invited both of them to come live with them.
By the time I got involved, Justin, Kristina, and their newborn son,
Jonathan, were living in a two-bedroom condo with Rick, Julie, and
their two-year-old child.

Justin and Kristina were not sure what they wanted to do, in terms
of their relationship. They were not married, they had dropped out of
high school, and they were going to try to raise their son together.
They had no real plan. This is not a couple who plans well. They are

both smart people, but they were young and did not have good support for making important life decisions.

From a professional point of view, I feared that they might be headed toward alcoholism. They hung out with a hard-partying bunch. Alcoholism in teenagers is often masked, because they're still young enough to drink a lot and yet have the energy to get out of bed and function.

For three months, Kristina and Justin tried to parent on their own. But they became increasingly miserable—particularly Kristina. They didn't have the maturity, for one thing, to care for a little baby, nor did they have the money to provide for the baby and themselves. Both of them were working at minimum wage jobs in a very expensive part of the world and were just not able to make any financial progress.

Meanwhile, I was monitoring the situation. As their pastor, I was providing what support I could. I never thought they might release the child to me. I was not looking to adopt a baby.

My wife, Holly, and I had lost a baby five years earlier, which was a very traumatic experience for us. We lost several babies through miscarriages, but this one was a stillbirth, born on his due date. It's devastating to lose a baby. We had set up the nursery and named him and were all ready to welcome him into our family. After he died, we got pregnant again, but lost that baby, too. We then went through pre-liminary in vitro procedures, but it was becoming clear to us that we were unlikely to produce any more children. We already had a beautiful little girl, Claire, who was eight years old, and we had always hoped for more children. By this time, however, I had put to rest the notion of having any more children. In my mind, my family consisted of me and Holly and Claire and I had learned to be content with that.

I was concerned, as well, for Holly. Obviously, her experience had been different from mine. She had carried our son for nine months and formed a bond with him that I, as a father, can never fully appreciate. As difficult as this journey through grief had been for me, I knew it was even more intense for Holly.

She would bring up the possibility of adoption now and again, but this was always a difficult conversation for me. I had made peace with the loss of our babies and I did not have the emotional energy to awaken that hope again. I was also concerned that Holly was still grieving over our losses, not only of our son, but also the loss of hope at ever producing another child. I was wary of adoption because I was not sure whether it would simply mask her grief and leave unfinished business, which I didn't think would be a healthy thing.

It's not that I didn't have any interest in adoption. As a matter of fact, the possibility of adopting from teenage birth parents had already crossed our horizon a couple of years earlier, when my cousin's son had a baby out of wedlock. He and his girlfriend got pregnant and were making an adoption plan. Someone in my family suggested that Holly and I might want to adopt that baby. My first response was that it would be too complicated, in terms of the family system. While I was still processing the idea, I heard that they had already found a family, so the question did not become a living issue for us. But the point is, I had already engaged a lot of the questions about what an open adoption might be like. I had lived it in my imagination. So by the time Justin and Kristina came into my life, I was warmed up to the notion of an open adoption. I had already worked through many of the issues.

Kristina and Justin had their baby in October and moved in with Rick and Julie. At that time, Julie came to me and asked, "Is there a possibility that you and Holly would adopt this baby, if this doesn't work out?"

I told her, "I'm open to anything, but please don't talk about this with Holly."

I tend to stay in a professional mode when I talk with my parishioners, so Julie's question really didn't affect me on an emotional level. I have to set certain emotional boundaries in my work, to maintain healthy relationships with my parishioners. I was simply counseling with Rick and Julie about their struggles, because it wasn't an easy living situation, with all of them together in one small apartment. And when I saw Justin and Kristina at church, I was always supportive.

Meanwhile, Holly had begun to see a therapist, who diagnosed her with Post Traumatic Stress Syndrome. Every time Holly would visit the gynecologist or the maternity ward of the hospital, she would get very anxious. She is a very self-aware person, and she recognized that she was developing some kind of phobia centered around hospitals and babies, so she went to talk to a therapist about it.

Holly's diagnosis helped her to name some of the stuff that she hadn't been able to name before. She made some rather dramatic breakthroughs related to the loss of our babies. It's not that she hadn't been aware that she was grieving her loss, but for some reason, she had never completed the grieving process. She knew she was hurting, but she still had to wake up in the morning and be a good mother to Claire and go to work and do all the things a person has to do in a day. It had been a tough five years for her.

Now she calls it her "Journey to Jonathan." But of course, in the middle of it, you can't see the end of the journey. I saw a marked change in Holly as a result of her conversations with her therapist. And I found it interesting that she wasn't talking about adoption anymore, which I took as a good sign that she was working on the right things. She wasn't looking for an easy fix. She was being healed before my eyes, and her progress made me feel more open to the possibility of adopting.

In December, Julie reported, "Kristina and Justin are beginning to surrender. They're beginning to realize that they are not going to be able to parent this baby."

That's when I kicked in. I began to do some emotional work at that point, because I anticipated that Kristina and Justin might come to us and ask us to adopt their child. But I still didn't mention it to Holly, because I didn't want her to get her hopes up, only to be disappointed.

I was aware that Rick and Julie had always believed it would be best for Justin and Kristina to place the child with an adoptive family. But I didn't see that they were pressuring them in any way. I agreed with them, philosophically. My default position is that when unmarried teenagers have a baby, they should adopt it out, unless there is compelling evidence that they can provide a healthy family environment for that child.

In January, when Jonathan was almost three months old, Julie told me, "Kristina and Justin want you and Holly to adopt their baby."

I was ready. Adopting Jonathan was a solution in all kinds of ways, for all the people involved. Holly and I would get a baby. Claire would get a little brother, which I knew would thrill her. It would help Justin and Kristina move on with their lives. It would help Rick and Julie. And I believed it just might save Jonathan's life.

I recognized the addiction issues that were at work in Justin and Kristina, though they couldn't yet see it. I have a lot of experience with addiction issues, and I knew that by adopting Jonathan, we might literally save his life by sparing him from those issues. That wasn't my sole motivation, but it was part of the total picture. My motivation was to do right by my family, by Jonathan, by Justin and Kristina, by Rick and Julie. Did adopting this baby serve some deep emotional need that I had? No, not really. I did not need to adopt a baby to be a happily fulfilled, engaged human being in the world. But it's too simple to say it was just an act of service. My life has been completely transformed by the addition of Jonathan to our family.

The next day, Kristina and Justin came in to my office. Kristina said, "Kevin, we want you and Holly to adopt our baby. We've been watching you guys and we want Jonathan to grow up in your family. If you don't take our baby, I don't think I can give him up. Will you take him?"

This was deeply affirming to hear. It made me feel very proud of my wife and my daughter to think that these two teenagers perceived us worthy of adopting Jonathan. It was a humbling moment.

We had a long conversation, exploring all kinds of issues around adoption. Kristina and Justin were both fully engaged in the conversation. I was in pastoring mode, at that point, although the conversation involved me on a very personal level. I was more than willing to receive the child and love the child, but only if I could see that they were completely ready to give him to us. I wanted to be sure this wasn't an impulsive decision and that they were clear about what adoption meant. I wanted to see that they had done the work they needed to do around surrendering Jonathan, whom they clearly loved very much. I wanted to make sure they weren't being pressured into this decision. It had to be their choice—a good, clean decision.

They both agreed that they could not parent this child. They acknowledged the challenges they were faced with—the limited money, their lack of maturity, the difficult living situation. They were feeling beat up and tired. I felt a lot of compassion for them. What a heroic effort! They had tried so hard and given so much and yet were able to recognize that for the good of their baby, they had to let him go. Clearly, they loved their son and wanted to make the best decision they could for him. When I felt confident that they were ready to surrender Jonathan, I called Holly and asked her to come down to my office.

I had talked to Holly the previous night about the possibility of adopting Jonathan. It was the first she knew about it. I told her, "This is not a done deal, but I need to know how you feel, because they're coming in to talk to me tomorrow."

Holly was elated. She immediately said, "Yes!" as tears welled in her eyes at this unanticipated blessing. In fact, the name "Jonathan" means "gift of God," and that's exactly how Holly received the news.

Holly came down to my office and the four of us talked for another four hours. I wanted Holly to hear Kristina say that she was ready to give up the baby. We talked about what adoption would mean for all of us, and for Jonathan. "You understand," I said to Justin and Kristina, "that if we adopt Jonathan, he becomes our child, just as if Holly had given birth to him?" They clearly understood and we spent a lot of time discussing it.

Kristina asked, "Can we see him? Can we write him?"

I said, "Absolutely. Jonathan will always know that you and Justin are his birth parents. He will grow up knowing who you are."

After the four of us had talked out all the issues, I asked, "When do you want us to take him?"

Kristina looked up and said, "Now. Can you take him now? I'm ready."

This response took me by surprise. My mind raced to think of reasons why this might not be a good idea. There was nothing in my experience to know how to answer this question. I felt that if I were to stumble in this process, it would be right here, right now. Having no knowledge or precedent to fall back on regarding "the best thing to do," I simply followed my heart. I looked at Holly and I could see the answer in her eyes. So I said, "Yes, we will take him now."

All of this happened so quickly that my daughter had no idea that she might soon be a sister. I raced home before Kristina and Justin brought Jonathan and said, "Claire, I have something very important to tell you. You are going to have a baby brother."

"When?" she asked.

Before I could answer, I heard the car pull into our driveway.

"Right now," I said.

Claire was very supportive, very excited, and wise beyond her years. She said, "I'm only eight years old. You and mom are the bosses, so you know what's best. But you know I've always wanted a brother or sister, so I think this is great news!"

Just then, Holly walked in with Jonathan. Right behind them came Justin and Kristina, Rick and Julie, and Maly, my assistant priest. There in our living room, we had a "passing of the child." We took a lot of pictures and talked for a while. So the very day of our interview with Kristina and Justin, Jonathan came home to us. When people ask me how long it took for us to adopt a baby, I say, "Oh, about eight hours."

Everything changed, as soon as Jonathan entered our home. I felt exactly as I did when Claire was born. I said to myself, "Okay, now I'm responsible for this kid's life. I'm going to feed him and burp him and change his diaper and send him to college. He's going to learn to say 'Yes, sir!' and 'No, sir!' and I hope he'll learn to love his dad."

Just as I became Claire's dad the moment she was born, I became Jonathan's dad the moment he came into our home. I felt the shift. That was the moment of decision for me. The moment I stepped up to the task, it was mine. Jonathan was my son from that moment on.

To legalize the adoption, I went on the Internet and got the appropriate forms from the State of California, filled them out, walked down to the courthouse and filed them. Then I hired an independent adoption agent, who interviewed Kristina and Justin to make sure they were surrendering the baby freely, so he represented their interests. The State then sent someone to investigate us. They visited our home and talked to me and Holly and Claire. After the required waiting period of six months, I filed a court order to adopt Jonathan. On the appointed court date, we walked into the courthouse, said "I do swear..." and that was it. It's a fairly simple procedure, at least in

California. It's not easy—I had to do my homework—but it was a simple, step-by-step process.

Though we didn't make a formal contract with Kristina and Justin, our ongoing relationship hasn't been a problem. Until they moved away, we would meet occasionally, in a casual setting, so they could see Jonathan. That felt perfectly fine to me, perhaps because I am good at setting boundaries. I didn't want Justin and Kristina to ever be in a situation where they might feel like caregivers for Jonathan, so we always treated them more like welcome visitors than family. They still call us from time to time, to ask how Jonathan is doing. I expect they will always be part of our lives, because they are such an important part of Jonathan's life.

There's no difference between my feelings for my birth daughter and my adopted son. I'm their dad. It began with the decision I made to be Jonathan's dad, that day he came home to us. Up until that moment, it was just a possibility that I was open to. Then all of a sudden, it was real. It was my decision to be there, to step into the reality of being Jonathan's father, to live into that reality. And there's no going back past that commitment. I'm his dad. He's my son. I love him to death. That's the reality.

Debbi

"It always amazes me to hear horror stories of adoption, because for me, it's been the most natural thing in the world. Every part of the whole experience has been perfect."

I decided to adopt because I'd always wanted a child. When I turned forty-one and was still single, I had to decide how much this meant to me. It was beginning to feel like a "now or never" thing. And it was becoming an issue with some of the men that I dated, those that didn't want children. I told a friend how much I wanted a child and he said, "Then I don't understand why you don't just have a child."

His comment spurred me to action. I realized I wanted a child more than anything, so I read a lot of books and did a lot of research. There was nobody in my life that I wanted to have a baby with and I didn't want to go some of the other routes, just to have a biological child. I couldn't quite get beyond the thought of telling my child, "Your father was Sperm A." And I didn't see the need for that. Adoption made sense to me. It was a completely natural thing for me to finally decide, "I will have a child through adoption."

I sat on the decision for six months, which is not my style. Usually, I make a decision and then immediately go for it. But this was big. I had to go through the process of deciding what kind of child I wanted and where to find her. I did know that I wanted a newborn girl. Everybody has some issue, something they are most concerned about in adopting a child. Some people don't want to do the whole baby thing, so they choose an older child. Others don't want to deal with transracial issues or special needs. For me, it was the physical health of the child. I realized I had to be completely honest with myself in this process of deciding what I could handle. Finding a healthy little girl was very important to me. Of course, you never know when something might happen, even with a birth child, but this was still a huge issue for me.

I also had to decide whether to do an international adoption or try to work out something domestically. As a single parent, international adoption is easier. Also, I thought I could get a healthier child internationally. And a lot of the domestic adoptions now are open adoptions and I'm not sure how I feel about that. Besides, I figured the odds were not in my favor as a single parent trying to adopt domestically. Fewer people would be likely to give their baby to a single mother, if they could find a suitable couple. So all of those considerations pushed me toward international adoption.

I chose an agency, got all my documents ready, and sent them to Guatemala in February. On March 14th, the agency called and announced, "You have a daughter. She was born yesterday and she is now at the foster home."

I was ecstatic! Just before the phone call, I had had a powerful feeling that this was totally right, that I was making the right decision to adopt. To have my daughter born was such a wonderful experience, even though I wasn't there. Just to have her, to know she was mine, to know she was here—or at least there, in Guatemala—was the highlight of my life.

I bought a plane ticket and went to meet her three weeks later. My mom went with me. My family was totally supportive from the beginning. They all had the same concerns I did about her physical health, and on the plane ride to Guatemala, my mother said, "You know, the real reason I'm here is if there's anything wrong with that child, I'm not going to let you adopt her." I knew that, but I wasn't worried about it.

When I first saw my daughter, I knew she was perfect. She was the most amazing thing I'd ever seen! It all felt right. Within five minutes, my mother said, "She's perfectly fine. She's a perfect child."

That trip to Guatemala to meet her granddaughter was one of the best experiences of my mother's life. As for me, it couldn't have been any more perfect. I called my daughter Isabel and spent a lot of time with her. I wanted to be there to capture that brand new baby face. I didn't want to miss out on any part of her life. Obviously, I did, since she wasn't free to leave the country for another five months, but it was important to me to be there, to see for myself that she was well cared for.

I went back to Guatemala when Isabel was three months old. A friend came with me this time and we had Isabel stay in the hotel with us. We did some sightseeing and had a great trip. It was hard to leave my baby, but for me, visiting her was preferable to entirely missing her first few months of life.

It is a difficult time, not having your child with you while the two governments complete the legal process. It's stressful, but it helped me to see that she was in good care. I felt like I was doing everything I could to make sure she was all right. I had just sold my business, so I had the time and the resources to go visit her while I waited. I was grateful for that.

I went back the third time to bring her home. She was five-and-a-half months old. Having a baby in my life felt completely normal and natural to me, even during those first few days and weeks. I had led a very active life—working, traveling, going out a lot. People had warned me, "Your life is really going to change." But nothing could have seemed more natural to me than being a mother. It was totally wonderful and delightful. I took six weeks off work, but even after that, I didn't do much work for the first three months she was home. That was probably the happiest period of my life. For me, the transition to motherhood was simple.

When I adopted, I was very aware that I was a single parent. I told myself, "If I meet someone—great—but if I don't, that's the way it's going to be. I'm taking full responsibility." I couldn't imagine what it would be like to have a partner, to have someone else do part of the work. But then, I know a lot of couples that don't have an equal parenting partnership, anyway. The good thing about being a single parent is you get to decide how to raise your child. There's no conflict. So in some ways, it's easier.

I do think it's important for single people considering adoption to have good support systems in place. And you have to have your life fairly well organized already. Things happen and nothing stays the same, but I think those are the pieces you really need to have in place before you add a child to your life.

I have a great support system in my family and friends. I have a friend down the road with a girl the same age as Isabel, so we trade childcare sometimes. Mostly, Isabel and I do fine on our own. But one time, I got a horrendous flu and that was absolutely terrifying to me, because I was physically unable to care for my daughter. I had to farm her out to family members, just so I could be sick. I do think more about wills and things like that. I have to think about what will happen to Isabel if something happens to me. As a single parent, I have more of a responsibility to take care of myself, because Isabel has only me to depend on.

Babies are physically demanding, but not very complex. You take care of them, you love them, and that's it. As Isabel gets older and more demanding, it is getting harder, more complex. She is a very strong, determined girl, full of energy and life, which is great. I wouldn't want it any other way. But I am feeling more stretched. I'm busy all the time.

It's been interesting dating again, with Isabel in the picture. In a serious relationship, a child brings up all sorts of new questions. It requires more juggling, just to manage the logistics.

The men in my life play a very important role in my daughter's life, as well. I'm quite conscious of it, because I want her to have healthy relationships with men. My father and my brothers and my men friends are all important role models for her. Isabel is starting to worry about not having a father. She'll say to me, "You have a dad, but I don't have a dad." I think that concerns her more right now than the cultural differences between us. People make comments—I suppose because we look different—but it always surprises me, because I don't notice it until somebody says something. By now, I feel like Isabel is totally mine, so I don't see any difference.

People are usually just curious and they don't mean any harm, but their comments do bother me. Even strangers will ask, "Where is she from?" I always say, "She's from Portland. Do you mean, 'Where was she born?'" Then I'll direct the question to Isabel so she can become a part of it, and she'll scream out, "Guatemala!"

At this point, she's insensitive to it, but I do worry about the prejudice she is likely to experience. I don't want her hurt. I want to protect her. But all I can do is help her develop a strong self image, so that she feels good about herself and proud of herself. She'll need to integrate who she is as an American with her Guatemalan background, and I don't quite know how to do that.

I do try to keep her connected to her cultural heritage. She is enrolled in the Spanish immersion program at our public school, for instance. But I also want her to feel completely secure about her connection to me and to our extended family. Also, I think she needs to feel that she's a part of the whole culture, that she feels like a legitimate American. She's a secure girl. She has good self esteem. I think as long as I can nurture that and help her maintain that pride and confidence in herself, she'll be okay.

One of the things that makes it easier for our children now is that they grow up with children and families that are all different. There are all kinds of families, with all kinds of ethnic makeup. That's much different—and much healthier—than the way it was when I was young, when there was one basic family model.

I know a little bit about Isabel's birth mother, but I don't know anything about her birth father. Her mother simply couldn't afford to keep her. The attorney that handled the adoption in Guatemala knew the birth mother. She told me that she was a very nice woman, very refined. I never did get to meet her. It's an amazing thing to think that the most important person in the world to me has this vital connection to a woman in Guatemala that neither of us is ever likely to know. At first, I felt a very strong connection to Isabel's birth mother. I felt very grateful to her for the amazing gift she gave me. I still feel that gratitude, and I am a bit sad that she doesn't get to see her daughter grow up. But I also feel that Isabel is totally my child now, so it's a different feeling than it was at first, during that transition period.

Sometimes I wish Isabel had a sibling. I would love to give her one, but I don't see a second adoption happening. I'm getting too old, and there's no way I could juggle everything so that the children received proper care. It's just the reality of my life, and I'm not really sad about it. At first, I craved another baby, but I'm beyond that now. There are so many other things going on in life. Even though I've loved every stage of Isabel's life, I look back and think, "Boy, that was a lot of work!" The only part that makes me sad about not adopting again is that Isabel won't have a sibling and I think she would enjoy that.

Adopting Isabel was definitely the best thing I've ever done. It's what makes my life rich. It always amazes me to hear horror stories of adoption, because for me, it's been the most natural thing in the world. Every part of the whole experience has been perfect. That's not to say that sometimes things aren't stressful or difficult, but I don't think it could be any more perfect. It's been a wonderful experience, the highlight of my life.

Cody

"I think anyone who gives their child up for adoption always wonders if they did the right thing."

Jenipher was seventeen and I was eighteen when we found out she was pregnant. I was pretty much at a loss as to what we were going to do, because we weren't stable. Jenipher was still in high school, but she started going to night school when she got pregnant. We were living with her mom and I was working at McDonalds. It was not a good situation.

We both agreed that abortion was not an option. And I didn't feel comfortable giving up the child and never knowing anything about what was happening in his life. So we decided we would keep him. I got a second job delivering pizza, because my initial reaction was, "I've got to earn enough money to support us." It was scary, though, because it wasn't enough.

Jenipher had a lot of back pain and couldn't even walk, so she stayed home most of the time. One day, when she was seven months pregnant, I came home from work and she started telling me about a show that Oprah Winfrey had done that day on open adoption. I didn't know anything about open adoption. Jenipher was rambling on, like pregnant women do, until I finally said, "What are you saying?"

She asked me, "Do you really think we are financially able to care for a child?"

I said, "No, that's why I'm working two jobs."

"But even with that, do we have the money? We've always thought there were only two options—abortion or keeping the baby. Here's a third option."

It only took us a week to find an agency that did open adoptions and to do the paperwork. Then we started looking through the books of prospective parents. We were picky about the parents we wanted. We wanted a stable home, one that was financially secure, with no other kids or pets, so that when we gave them our baby, their whole focus would be on that child. Maybe it was selfish of us, but that's what we were looking for.

One couple really stood out from the rest, so we decided to meet them. I wasn't sure what open adoption was going to be like, and I still felt like I would be losing the baby. It was very scary. I told Jenipher, "How do we know these people are what they say they are? They can tell us anything they want, but what happens when they take our baby home?"

When we met Mike and Mary Alice for the first time, that's what we were most concerned about. We talked for about an hour and a half, and I just felt an honesty in them. They were very open. Jenipher was asking subtle questions, trying to get into their personal lives, and we were both listening to see if they really were who they said they were. She and I had discussed beforehand certain signals that we would use to communicate with each other, like squeezing the other person's hand if something felt bad or wrong. But neither of us had to do that. The counselor finally asked us if we would like to talk privately, but we just looked at each other and knew. I said, "No, I don't need any time." Jenipher said, "We're ready. Do we need to sign anything now?"

We wrote up a contract, about visitations and other contact, which was a stressful process for me. But Mary Alice noticed my anxiety and said, "It's just a formality. Trust me, we probably won't even go by it, so you guys put in whatever you want." As it turns out, that contract has meant absolutely nothing in terms of our relationship over the past twelve years, but I suppose the agency needed it for their files. We've just worked it all out between us, like friends.

It was June, and unusually hot. I was off work one day and Jenipher wanted to go cool off in some water, so we drove out to the river, waded across to a little pool, and sat in the water. She was not yet eight months pregnant, and I was teasing her about her water breaking while she was sitting there in the river when she suddenly looked at me in alarm and said, "We'd better go. I think my water just broke, but I can't really tell."

While I gathered up our things, Jenipher started having contractions. I was holding everything in one arm and holding her up with the other arm, and we waded back across the river to the car. Jenipher was in a panic, but I was feeling quite calm. She kept yelling, "How can you be so calm? I'm in labor!" I just kept repeating, "Everything's going to be okay." As we sped back toward town, I called the hospital on the cell phone to tell them we were on our way.

We had talked about having Mike and Mary Alice there at the birth, but we opted not to have anyone else there, because this was going to be the only time the child was actually ours. However, they were waiting in the hospital when our son was born, twenty-six hours later.

It was exciting to watch my first son being born. At that precise moment, I wasn't sure I was making the right choice. I knew I was making the right choice for the child, but I wasn't sure it was right for me. We chose adoption for the sake of our child, not for us. That's the only reason we did what we did, because we knew we couldn't provide what we wanted to provide for our child. We weren't stable ourselves, so how could we bring a third person into the mix and expect that to make us stable?

The day after the birth was actually the hardest. The reality of it began to sink in. Jenipher had just given birth, yet we had no baby. We had to sign a zillion papers, which was hard, because we thought we were done with all that. Then we went home and we both got in the shower and just stood there and cried for half an hour.

Mike and Mary Alice named the baby Mitchell and we had no contact with them until September. They were waiting for us to call, because that was part of the original contract. Jenipher had decided that she didn't want to see the baby for the first year. She thought it would be too hard. That's not really how I felt, but I knew that since the baby had come from her body, it would probably be harder for her, and I understood that.

Jenipher initiated that first visit. She called Mike and Mary Alice and said, "I need to see him."

They said, "Great. Where do you want to meet?"

We met in a park on a beautiful sunny day. When I first saw my son, tears of joy sprang to my eyes because he looked so healthy and I could see that they were taking good care of him. At that point, I knew I had made the right choice. I had wondered, up until then. I think anyone who gives their child up for adoption always wonders if they did the right thing. You question yourself. "Did I really do it for the child? Did I do it for me? Why *did* I do it?" But that first visit made me really happy. I felt much more peaceful about the whole thing.

Jenipher and I ended up getting married and we have two more children now. Our relationship with Mitchell and his parents is very open and trusting. I don't actually talk to them very often. I'm not much of a conversationalist. But Jenipher talks to Mary Alice more than I think I even know about. She says there's no one word to describe Mary Alice. Jenipher says she's like a best friend, a mom, an aunt, and a sister all rolled into one person.

As it turned out, Mary Alice got pregnant about four years after our son was born, after fifteen years of trying. So now Mitchell has a little sister. At first, I was really concerned. I wondered if they would treat their adopted son in the same manner that they would their biological daughter. One of the reasons we picked them was because they had no kids, so we were both worried about it. But we've watched them over the past eight years with the two kids, and there hasn't been any change at all in the way they treat Mitchell. They treat both of their children with the same love and regard.

As a matter of fact, Mary Alice called us a few months after her daughter was born, worried that we would try to get Mitchell back. We went over to their house and talked it through. We told them, "No, of course we won't try to take him back. That was never the plan. We would never have given him to you, just to try to take him back. Besides, we can't. We've signed away all rights to him, so there's nothing we could do, even if we wanted to. Which we don't." I guess they had their own concerns about the new situation.

Jenipher usually sets up our visits and I tag along. We visit at his house or go to the park. We'll have dinner with their family, or I'll take Mitchell out and show him some soccer moves, since I'm a soccer player and he really likes the game. I look for those things in him— who he looks like, what he likes to do.

Mike and Mary Alice are always open to whatever we want to do. We recently asked them if we could take Mitchell fishing and camping with us. Mary Alice responded, "That would be great, because Mitchell likes to fish, but we don't, so that would be good for him to go with you."

It's always like that. Whenever we want to see him, they are more than willing. We go see him on his birthday, and at Christmas, we take presents. Just normal family events. Sometimes we bring our kids with us, and all four of the kids—theirs and ours—behave like brothers and sisters. It's like we've combined two different families into one giant family. That's what it feels like.

Because we chose such great parents for our son in the beginning, there haven't been any major challenges along the way. I know there are some moments coming up, as Mitchell moves into adolescence. He knows his whole story, so everything is out in the open. But I know that questions may come up for him. He may ask, "Why did you give me up for adoption? Why me, and not my brother and sister?" And that scares me. I'm just going to be completely honest with him. I'll tell him, "We couldn't provide for you the way your parents have. It's not that we love you any differently. There's absolutely no difference in how we feel about you. It was purely situation and timing." That's going to be a hard thing to explain to him. It was such a hard thing for us to do, but I hope he understands that we did it because we love him.

It never occurred to me to run, not even when I first found out Jenipher was pregnant. Not only was I committed to her, but my father raised me to stand up for myself and to take responsibility for my actions. So when she said, "I'm pregnant," I responded, "*We're* pregnant." Just because the woman is the only one that can produce doesn't mean she's the only one that is responsible. It doesn't mean that it is her problem or her fault. I couldn't imagine not sticking around to see it through, because I had a sense that things weren't as bad as they appeared, that there might be some gifts in this experience.

I don't know that I would change anything that's happened. Sure, it's been hard, but some of the greatest joys of my life have come through this experience. It's not only that Mitchell is a person now, it's what we were able to provide for someone else. We gave the gift of life—to Mitchell *and* to his parents—and there's no greater gift than that. And because we loved our son so much, we gave him the best gift we could—a wonderful family who can provide everything he needs.

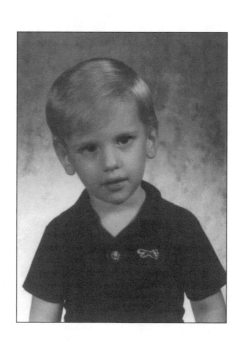

Barbara

"I had a clear confirmation that Joe was mine, and when you know that about a child, it doesn't matter whether they come from your body or not. They are you. They are your heart."

My husband, Don, and I tried to have children soon after we were married, but we quickly discovered that we had infertility issues. It took us four years to conceive our first son, Scott. When Scott was two years old, I went to a fertility specialist and said, "We are ready to have another baby. It took us a long time the first time, so we want to get started on this one now."

The doctor told me, "You've had all the tests and you know that the odds are not in your favor for conceiving another child. You need to think about adoption."

"No," I replied, "I think I'll go find myself a lover with a health card and a high sperm count, because I'm not ready to do an adoption."

What neither of us knew that day was that I was already two weeks pregnant. During my pregnancy, I worked in a hospital, and I always wondered what that doctor thought when he saw me. I guess he thought I found a suitable lover pretty quickly!

After our daughter was born, I never conceived again, though not for lack of trying. Then my uterus prolapsed and I had a hysterectomy, so that was the end of that.

I knew we were supposed to have another baby. I knew it so strongly I was even producing colostrum. I told my husband, "We have another baby," but he just patted me on the head and said, "There, there. You go through this every once in a while. It will be all right."

But I knew there was a baby out there that was meant to be ours. So I went about the business of trying to find my child. My husband was supportive, though passive. He saw it as my quest, as something I needed to do, but he did not share the same vision or desire. To me, it felt like a mission. Even though I had two children already, it was like I kept counting chicks and coming up one short.

I started talking to people, like everybody does who begins this journey. I talked to a couple of attorneys who handled adoptions in Florida; I talked to the State and took their classes; I talked to others who had adopted; I talked to a church agency. I just started following the path, trusting that it would lead me to my child. People told me, "You open doors and just let things happen." I still believe that. All you can do is open doors and let things happen.

I applied for adoption through the State of Florida. I also contacted LDS Family Services. But the counselor who met with me there told me, "I've been with this agency eight years and there's never been a child born here that you are qualified for. Because you already have two healthy children, we have to put you in the 'special needs' category. I'll give you the paperwork, but don't hold your breath." The date was September 2nd. Joe was born two days later.

I went home and put the paperwork on a shelf. It stayed there for seven weeks. Nothing happened. Then one night, Don and I were at a Boy Scout function and I met a woman there who was a volunteer at LDS Family Services. She told me, "We've had a baby boy born that you might be interested in. If so, you'd better turn in your paperwork." She couldn't give me any more information than that. The next day, I completed all the papers and handed them in to the agency.

Meanwhile, miracles were unfolding. I was working full-time, but I began to feel that I ought to quit. I had attended a church conference in June, where mothers had been counseled to stay home with their young children, if at all possible. I really took that to heart, and because I recognized it as a spiritual response, I acted on it. I turned in my resignation.

Without my income, we couldn't afford to stay in the house we lived in, so we put it on the market. It still hadn't sold by November, when I turned in the adoption paperwork. A few days after the agency received our papers, they called us in for an interview. Our financial statement looked pitiful, because the house hadn't sold and I had no job, and as the social worker looked it over, she said, "These numbers don't add up."

A few days later, I asked Don, "Who told you we were being transferred to Tallahassee?"

He said, "What are you talking about?"

"You told me you were being transferred to Tallahassee by January 1st," I replied. The point of my question was that it would change our plans for buying a house locally, if he were being transferred.

Don said, "You're nuts. I never told you that."

Within three days, the house sold, Don got transferred to Tallahassee—with a pay raise—and we got Joe.

The agency called us in again to look at pictures. We still didn't have much information about this baby, so I was eager to see the photos. My husband was still very passive, but he went along with me because he knew how important this was to me. A social worker named Mike met with us and he asked Don, "Are you willing to take a child and raise it as your own?"

Don said, "I support my wife in this decision."

Mike asked again, "Are you willing to take a child and raise it as your own?"

Don replied in the same manner, "I support my wife in this decision."

Mike repeated the question a third time, using the same words, and something changed in that moment. I was sitting in the corner and I could see Don's face. As a nurse, I've seen people's blood fall through their body, like a wash, and that's what seemed to happen to Don. His countenance literally changed. He looked at Mike and said, "I will do everything within my power to take care of this child and to raise him the way he deserves."

I just about fell out of my chair. The change in him was so sudden and so deep. Every time we had talked to a social worker before, Don had asked me, "What do you want me to say? I want to be sure I say the right thing." But this time, he was speaking straight from the heart. It was a pivotal moment and I knew it.

After I'd recovered a bit, I asked, "So now can we see the pictures?"

"Why do you want to see pictures?" asked Mike. "Don't you want to see the baby?"

"I didn't know that was an option. Where is he?" I asked.

"In the next room," Mike said, as he stood up to lead us there.

We walked into the adjoining room and there I met Joe for the first time. He was seven weeks old, but he had been born prematurely, so he was a long, skinny baby with a long, narrow face. He looked pathetic. He had had a depressed skull fracture when he was born, so they had shaved one half of his head and I could see a tiny scar where they had operated to elevate his skull. He had a lot of hair, at least on one side of his head. I looked at him hesitatingly, wondering what we were getting ourselves into.

Mike asked, "So do you want him?"

I said, "I think so." But I was thinking, "He looks like a little shrunken man."

I picked up that little shrunken man and took him home. We had gone to look at photographs and had come home with a baby. We had nothing. No crib, no clothes, no money. We didn't even have the money for the adoption fee, which at that time, was $1,750. It might as well have been $17,000. But the miracles continued.

I borrowed a car seat from the agency, strapped the baby in, and headed home. On the way, I stopped at a store and spent our grocery money on diapers, tee-shirts, rubber pants, and bottles. Don had gone home and called our neighbors, who had also adopted. By the time I got home, there was a crib set up in our house and a pile of baby clothes in the front room.

The adoption fee loomed over us, though we were too busy with a new baby to think much about how we were going to pay it. The very next day, I got a check in the mail. It was from a place I had worked at two years previously, and it came with a letter that explained, "We have audited our payroll records and found that you have been underpaid." That check was just enough to cover the adoption fee and the $100 I had spent the day before, plus an extra ten dollars.

I remember the shock of the whole experience. I would walk by the crib and look at baby Joe out of the corner of my eye and think the words that newly adoptive parents won't utter, "That's my baby." I kept telling my mind and my heart, "That's my son. I am his mother." I was trying to get the reality of it internalized. It doesn't take a long time, but at least for me, it was a conscious process. Within six months, I would have run to Timbuktu with him rather than let anyone take my son from me.

Social workers from the agency kept coming into our home for the post-placement visits. Now that I am a social worker and do the same kind of thing, I'm very aware that it is a necessary part of a legal adoption, but at the time, it felt like an ordeal I had to submit to. Those social workers represented a force that had the power to take my son from me, and that made me very anxious, at least for several months. I thought I had to look like the perfect mother.

I remember when things shifted for me, when I stopped worrying about what other people thought of my parenting. I was sitting in church with Joe one day and he started to fuss. I caught myself thinking, "People are watching. What do they think I should do? Take him out? Sit here and try to quiet him?" All of a sudden, I realized what I was doing and I chastised myself, "What the hell am I thinking? I just need to take care of my baby and not worry about what other people think." After that, I forgot all about worrying what others thought, even the social workers that were still in my life. I just took care of my children the best I could.

We moved to Tallahassee shortly after Joe came home. One day about three years later, Don went to work as usual and was killed in a plane crash. I was left with three children to care for. I did have a job at that time, but I was so devastated that I was unable to work. I went back to school, because I could just manage to be accountable to myself, though not to an employer. Don's death preoccupied me for about five years.

I married David several years later. There is a difference between being a divorcee and being a widow, when you bring children into a new relationship. My children had a father and they did not feel the need to replace him. It wasn't like he had run off with a redhead. He had simply died. Even though Joe refers to David as "Dad" when he is talking to others, he has never called him "Dad" directly. They have a good relationship, but it's not a real father/son relationship.

I don't think Joe has any real issues about being adopted. I don't even think he thinks of himself as adopted. We've had birth children in our home, then Joe, plus twenty foster kids, and I've never treated any of them differently. I felt no differently toward my biological kids than I did toward my adopted child, after that first six months of adjusting. Joe is my child. I had a clear confirmation that he was mine, and when you know that about a child, it doesn't matter whether they come from your body or not. They are you. They are your heart.

I have always told the children in my home, "Kids come in different ways. Some are born here, some are adopted, and some are fostered here. You are all children that have come to this home, and it doesn't matter how. You belong here."

As for me, I think there are those of us in the world who are extremely maternal, so much so that we can bond to a stone. We will bond to anyone, as much as people will let us. And that's how it's been with all the children who have come into my life.

I went into social work after Don died, and now I work as a professional in the adoption field. I work with birth parents and adoptive parents alike. I've done home studies and post-placement visits. I've helped birth parents find families for their children. I've done every piece of it.

I've been in hospitals with birth mothers and have been appalled at how society—especially the medical community—treats birth mothers. I've worked with girls through their entire pregnancy and then heard some horrendous comments from medical staff. I had one birth mother who was pregnant by rape—a stranger rape, at knifepoint. She was planning to place the baby for adoption and she had a boyfriend who was there with her to support her through the birth. After the baby was born, one of the nurses said, "You guys are so much in love. Why don't you get married and keep this baby?"

People make assumptions—huge assumptions, with far too little information. This nurse was making assumptions. She treated me horribly, because she considered me the bad person who was stealing the baby from this loving couple. Sometimes people's prejudices get in the way of their compassion and good sense.

Prejudices around mothers and infants run deep. Recently, I had a birth mother tell me, "I don't like my midwife." I was surprised, because midwives are usually the most compassionate. But in this case, when she found out the girl was planning an adoption, the midwife made disparaging comments about the girl's maternal instincts.

People don't realize the agony that birth mothers go through in making a decision to place a baby for adoption. It does not in any way mean they would not be good mothers. Every girl loves her baby, and adoption needs to be seen as a loving choice that is made at great cost. It is a painful, agonizing choice. It's hard for people to understand. They don't understand how someone could give up their baby. What they don't realize is that birth parents do it for love of the child.

Some birth fathers get involved, too. There is a lot of controversy over the rights of birth fathers. State laws vary widely on this. In some States, the birth father has to voluntarily step forward to be involved in the adoption process. He has to assert his rights. In other States, the law requires that the birth father's parental rights be legally terminated before an adoption can go through. This is not always easy. Casual sex happens all the time, and sometimes the guy doesn't even know the girl is pregnant. Sometimes the girl doesn't even know who the father is. In the States that require it, if we don't know who the father is, or we can't find him, we have to publish the facts we do know—which can be embarrassing—to give the birth father a chance to step forward before his rights are terminated by the court.

Some birth fathers get hurt along the way, no matter what is decided. In general, birth parents try to do what's best. I think they need to look at all their options and make a decision based on what's best for the baby and what's best for them. They need to gather information, put some real thought and even prayer into it, and make the best decision they can. Most agencies welcome birth fathers' involvement and give them the same opportunities that they offer birth mothers. No one purposely excludes birth fathers from the decision-making process, though they are often excluded by circumstance or choice.

Oftentimes, the extended family is also involved. The hardest thing for parents to do is let their children make their own decisions and to be supportive, regardless of what they decide. Parents strongly believe that they know what is best for their children—and very often, they do—but the point is, it's their journey. You have to let your children find their own way. If they choose to keep that child, you have to still be their parent, and yet not enable them. If they place that child, you still need to be the parent. If your children mess up, you still have to help them. This is one of the hardest parts of parenting. My grandma used to tell me, "When they're little, they pull on your apron strings, and when they're grown, they pull on your heart strings."

Almost everyone has their own personal experiences with adoption, so they come at it from their own point of view. When we adopted Joe, my father made a horrible comment. I called my parents as soon as Joe came home and announced, "We have a new baby." My dad was very nice on the phone, but he called back ten minutes later to ask, "Why do you think you need to do this? I raised my mistakes. Everybody should raise their own. Why do you think you need to raise someone else's bastard child?"

My dad wasn't trying to be mean. He had grown up during the Depression on a rural Alabama farm, when there was no birth control and families were large. Probably the last thing anybody wanted was another mouth to feed. That was simply his perspective. That's how most people with his background thought of it. You raised your own mistakes.

I responded, "Dad, I never knew you thought of us as mistakes. And Joe is not a bastard, because I am married." Then I didn't talk to him for three months. It was never mentioned again and my dad always treated Joe just fine, but I'm sure that first reaction was his heartfelt response. Our prejudices run deep and far, and most of the time, we're not even aware of them. It's just the way we see the world.

We have no relationship with Joe's birth parents. Twenty years ago, when he was born, they didn't give you much information. And Joe has never expressed an interest in searching for them. Because of his medical problems, I did request non-identifying information from the agency, which any adoptive parent can do.

As an adoptive mother, I am fine with a closed adoption. As a professional, I think both sides have to be in complete agreement about the degree of openness in their adoption plan. There should be a contract, right from the beginning. I see contracts as negotiable arrangements, but after they are agreed upon and signed, they are inflexible. The problem that I run into as an adoption counselor is that initially, adoptive parents are willing to do anything, but then they can't live it later. It's easy when a pregnant woman is telling you that she'll give you her baby if you'll agree to pictures or letters or visits or whatever. The adoptive parents are often not honest with themselves. Later, when they get the baby home, they become unwilling to share that baby. I understand that, but when you agree to something, you need to honor that agreement. The birth parents deserve that. Birth parents have all the chips before the birth, but after a placement, they have no bargaining power. I simply want people to do what they've agreed to do. I'm very adamant about that. I have no problem calling one of my adoptive couples and giving them blazes if they're not honoring the contract they made with the birth parents.

The adoption scene is changing fast. The Internet is having a huge impact, because people have access to so much information. A pregnant fourteen-year-old in Ohio can type in "adoption" on an Internet search engine and find loads of information. But I don't see State agencies, health departments, and school systems keeping up. They don't talk about adoption as an option, typically. I worked in a couple of school systems in the teen parenting program and during one semester, the students heard one speaker, for one hour, talk about adoption. In a whole semester, with seven hours of daily instruction!

Adoption doesn't get the dignity it deserves. Birth parents ought to be respected for being able to say, "I'm not prepared to parent this child, and that doesn't make me a horrible person." Adoption is a loving choice, for birth parents and adoptive parents alike. It gives that child a better opportunity, it gives the birth parents better opportunities, and it gives the adoptive parents an opportunity to have a more fulfilled life. Everyone benefits.

Acknowledgments

I always read the Acknowledgments, too. It reminds me that none of us can create anything all alone. And for a writer, creating a book is a useless endeavor without readers to receive it. So first and foremost, I thank you, my readers, for providing me the motivation to keep working during the many days I would rather have played in the sun or, on really desperate days, cleaned the house. This book is for you.

There is nothing more powerful than a parent who believes in you, and I am blessed with two terrific parents—Jean Simmons and Alan Meadows—who always believed I could accomplish whatever I dared dream. My brothers, Greg and Phillip, and especially my sister and next door neighbor, Kimberlee, have been true friends throughout my life.

Marge and Wayne Phillips provided unwavering support and a peaceful place to retreat when I most needed it. Muriel Knight, my fun-loving great-aunt, lets me bunk with her during the Maui Writers Conference. My good friend, Donna Kelly, sparked the idea for this book, and as always, June Collier has been my faithful and trusted friend throughout. Tracey Snoyer, Patti Rokus, and Janet Cook inspire me to keep reaching for Truth. Kelly Hale, Anita Compton, Maria Solorio, and the great team at the Eagle Point Community Bible Church Daycare took good care of my kids while I worked. And to the members of my first writing group—Anna Mays, Judy Simmons, Laura Steenhoek, Tom Cutts, and Susan Conner-Griffin—you are in my heart forever.

My husband, Stephen, is my best friend and ever loyal support. He's a great parenting partner, which may account for the fact that our six children—Garrett, Gordon, Genevieve, Gabrielle, Grace, and

Gloria—are totally amazing people. I am continually and gratefully astounded at my good fortune to be the mother of such strong and gifted souls.

Finally, and most importantly, this book could not have happened without the selfless contribution of those who shared their adoption stories with me. Many of the interviews were tearful affairs, as we explored difficult memories and deep emotions. Thank you to all those who trusted me to tell their story with honesty and heart. This is your book.

Do you have an adoption story to share?

If you've picked up this book, you probably do. I am always interested in hearing other adoption experiences. Sharing our stories with each other creates a community like no other. If you would like to share your adoption story or that of someone you know, visit my website, send me an e-mail or a fax, or send it via snail mail. You don't have to be a great writer to tell a great story. (That's what editors are for!) Be sure to include full contact information. Who knows? You may be in my next book!

Lisa Garfield
c/o Agate Lake Publishing
P.O. Box 2164
White City, OR 97503
fax: 775-261-5609
e-mail: lisagarfield@peoplepc.com
website: ForLoveOfAChild.com

Do you know someone who would enjoy
For Love of a Child: Stories of Adoption?

Please send _____ copies of *For Love of a Child: Stories of Adoption* at $14.95 USD each, plus $4 shipping for 1 book, $2 each additional.

_____ Please send an autographed copy for only $1 extra. (Enclose desired inscription.)

_____ Please gift wrap my copy for an extra $2. (Enclose gift tag instructions.)

Name _____

Address _____

_____

Email _____

_____ My check or money order for $_____ is enclosed.

_____ Please charge my credit card: ____Visa ____Mastercard

Card number _____

Expiration _____

Signature _____

Make your check payable and return to:
Agate Lake Publishing
P.O. Box 2164
White City, OR 97503
OR: Call in your credit card order to: 877-830-0811
Order online at: ForLoveOfAChild.com
Fax your order to: 775-261-5609
For bulk orders, call for discount schedule.

Check my website for new products, events, and information:
www.LisaGarfield.com

WARNER MEMORIAL LIBRARY
EASTERN UNIVERSITY
ST. DAVIDS, PA 19087-3696